DISHES TO DIVE FOR

Burntisland Heritage Trust
Scottish Charity No. SC028539

Somerville Street, Burntisland
Illustration courtesy of Anna Briggs

First published October 2000 by Burntisland Heritage Trust.
Printed by: McGilvray Printers, Kirkcaldy.

ISBN 0 9539353 0 2

Price: £8.99

ACKNOWLEDGEMENTS

Burntisland Heritage Trust gratefully acknowledges all the people who took the time and the trouble to make gastronomic contributions to this book. The response from Local and National Celebrities has been excellent and their contributions have been gratefully received. A listing of these Celebrities is given on the inside front cover. Thanks also to all other contributors without whom this book would have been considerably thinner!! Any delays in the publication of this book have been entirely due to some members of the Trust insisting that they try the recipes first. Some of the recipes had to be tried at least twice before they were sure they were all right, at least that's their excuse.

Particular thanks are due to:
Stewart and Hazel Simpson, without whose inspiration and tenacity this book would never have found its way to the kitchen.
The Friends of Burntisland Heritage Trust whose help in the compilation of this book was invaluable.
Cluny & Cromarty for their humour and artwork.
Anna Briggs, Alan Barker and John M Pearson for allowing us to use their illustrations.
Eric Bell for allowing us to use his painting titled "The Blessing of Burntisland" as the basis of our logo.
Frank Baird for the design and production of the book cover and his assistance and support in the collation and presentation of the book.
Ian Quinney for his computer skills, determination and calming influence.
Gavin Anderson Photography for the photograph that graces the back cover. (Technical data: subject at 3 ft. distance, camera settings 12mm lens, F8, twin strobes on manual with full power to balance ambient light.)
Robert Wharton of W. D. Wharton Publishers, Wellingborough for assisting with the technical aspects of publishing.
Thalia Teasdale for her excellence in proof reading.
McGilvray Printers for their patience and help.

Also grateful thanks go to the following companies and groups for their monetary donations or goods in kind that helped to get this project off the ground.

Inveresk Paper Mill
Shell U.K. Exploration and Production
Exxon Chemical Olefins Inc.
Alcan Chemicals Europe
The Rotary Club of Burntisland & Kinghorn

Should you wish further information on the Charles wRex Project or any aspect of Burntisland's rich and varied history, please contact us at 4 Kirkgate, Burntisland, Fife, Scotland, KY3 9DB or visit our website www.kingcharles-wrex.co.uk.

All proceeds from the sale of this recipe book will benefit Burntisland Heritage Trust; a non-profit making charitable organisation dedicated to keeping Burntisland's heritage alive.

FOREWORD

In 1633, after he had been crowned King of Scotland, Charles I went on a coronation tour of royal palaces. On his way back to Edinburgh it had been arranged for his baggage carts to be transported in two ferries across the Firth of Forth between Burntisland and Leith. Shortly after leaving Burntisland on 10 July, one of the ferries containing many of the King's personal and household items sank in a sudden squall.

Following several unsuccessful commercial attempts to locate the wreck between 1992 and 1995, a local project team was set up under the auspices of Burntisland Heritage Trust to continue the search. From the outset the present team has made it clear that, if successful, any resources generated (including artefacts recovered) would be donated to the nation.

In December 1998 a portfolio of evidence which indicated the presence of a wooden vessel buried in the seabed off Burntisland was presented to Historic Scotland. The local search team collated the data over a 12-month period from a number of sources, including the Royal Navy. Prior to the fieldwork a Lancashire map dowser, Mr Jim Longton, had pinpointed the location.

In the autumn of 1999 a young diver surfaced from his first dive on the designated wreck site. His first comment to me at that time was that it was a miracle that in such conditions any wreck discovery had been made at all. He was right. The remains of the wooden shipwreck lie completely buried, at least five feet below the mud and silt. The seabed is almost flat except for two slightly raised parallel ridges. On most of the high-water dives, at a depth of eighty-four feet, the diver is lucky if he can see more than a few feet. More details and background can be found on our website at: **www.kingcharles-wrex.co.uk**

In many ways the word 'miracle' describes the whole project. Twenty years ago the discovery would not have been possible, but leading edge technology today has given us an advantage. There is however more to it than just science. To me the real 'miracle' has been the bonding of a small group of dedicated people united by a common cause. These range from divers to businessmen; scientists, historians and archaeologists; fund-raising volunteers and even humorists. The project has received enormous support in kind and assistance but there is an ongoing need for funds to resource this work and it is hoped that the initiative of this book will go a long way to providing much needed financial support.

I would like to thank you for buying this book and hope that you enjoy the recipes and the humour.

Ian Archibald
Project Manager

CONTENTS

Burntisland Coat of Arms
Courtesy of Burntisland Community Council

Conversion Tables

Solid Weight Conversion

Metric	Imperial
15g	½oz
30g	1oz
55g	2oz
115g	4oz
170g	6oz
225g	8oz
340g	12oz
455g	16oz

Liquid Volume Conversion

Metric	Imperial
30ml	1fl oz
55ml	2fl oz
115ml	4fl oz
140ml	5fl oz
170ml	6fl oz
225ml	8fl oz
285ml	10fl oz
425ml	15fl oz
570ml	20fl oz

Metric equivalents rounded to nearest 5 units.
Data courtesy of Alan Hamilton, Trading Standards Service of Fife Council.

Weights dated 1826 and measures dated 1860.
These were originally kept in the Old Tollbooth located at the bottom of the High Street 1616-1843 and were used to ensure fair-trading.

Photograph courtesy of Stewart Simpson

Prior to 1824, in which year the Imperial Bushel was adopted as the standard,
there were several different measuring systems in use throughout the country.

On display
½ gallon, ½ peck, 1 peck, ½ bushel, 1 bushel
28 lb weight, 56 lb weight

1 bushel = 8 gallons
= 4 pecks
= 36.4 litres

Grateful thanks to Alan Hamilton, Trading Standards Service of Fife Council
for his assistance in researching these historic measures.

Granny Jean's Scotch Broth

Cromarty's Hame-made Broth
Was renowned baith near and far,
Mair popular than wine or ale,
In monies a pub and bar.
Sustaining and uplifting,
A brew baith fine and grand,
It brought spirit for the body,
An' fame throughout the land.

'Twas Granny's secret recipe
That made it a success,
An! whit she tippled in till't,
Mony tried tae guess.
But nane could ever match it,
Caw as tho' they may,
But they never fund the secret.
That is, until today.

A couthy, canty, country quine,
Jeannie had her wiles,
An' what she lacked in fine finesse,
She made up for, in style.
So let us raise oor soup spoons,
An' Jeannie's name exalt,
For her paucity wi' stock cubes,
An' her fondness o' the Malt.

©Cluny & Cromarty MM

Devilled Mushroom Cups

Hazel Simpson - Heritage Trust Volunteer

Ingredients - Serves 4

1 tablespoon Worcestershire sauce
1 teaspoon tomato purée
salt and ground pepper
2 tablespoons soured cream
4 sprigs of chervil, to garnish

4 large, thin slices of white bread
3 oz melted butter
2 oz pickling onions
1 thick gammon steak, cut into short sticks
8 oz mushrooms, chopped

Method

Preheat the oven to 200ºC/400ºF/gas mark 6

Use a large biscuit cutter to stamp the bread into rounds. Soak the rounds in 2 oz of the melted butter and use to line 4 tartlet moulds. Put an empty tray on top to hold the bread in shape as it cooks. If you don't have a second tartlet tray, cover the buttered bread cases with greaseproof paper and fill with rice to hold them down. Bake for 10 minutes, then remove the top tray or greaseproof paper and rice. Bake for a further 10 minutes to allow the bottoms to brown and become crispy.

Meanwhile make the filling: fry the onions and gammon in the remaining 1 oz butter until lightly browned. Add the mushrooms and fry quickly at first to brown them, then turn the heat down and cook slowly until all the mushroom juice has evaporated. Gently stir in the Worcestershire sauce, tomato purée and salt and pepper to taste. Fill the toast shells with the filling mixture then spoon the soured cream over the top. Garnish with the chervil sprigs and serve.

This dish can be made in advance: reheat the toast shells and filling separately, then assemble just before serving.

Cooking time: 15 minutes

Watercress Soup

The Hon. Mrs. Frances Shand Kydd

Ingredients - Serves 6

2 bunches (or pkts) watercress
1 medium sized onion
1 oz butter
1 lb potatoes
1½ pints chicken stock

1 bay leaf (optional)
pinch of grated nutmeg
salt and freshly milled pepper
2-3 tablespoons single cream
½ pint milk

Method

Melt the butter on low heat, add chopped onion and fry gently for 5 minutes until soft, not brown.

Add the stock, sliced potatoes, bay leaf and seasoning. Bring to the boil, then add half the watercress and simmer for 15 minutes (till the potatoes are tender). Draw off heat and discard cooked watercress and the bay leaf and stir in the milk. Chop the remaining watercress or preferably use food processor and seal wrap in a small bowl.

Put all the cooked ingredients in food processor and liquidize. Pour it back into the pan, heat gently to the boil, then add the uncooked watercress and cream and serve immediately. The soup can be cooked beforehand and the uncooked watercress and cream added at the last minute.

This recipe can be used for spinach or parsley in the same way.

Cooking time: 30 minutes

Cream of Chicken Soup with Lemon and Tarragon

Cathie McKendrick - Wishaw

Ingredients - Serves 6

1½ oz butter
1 medium onion, finely chopped
4 oz chicken breast cut into small pieces
2 teaspoons dried tarragon
1 oz plain flour

1 pint vegetable stock
grated rind and juice of 1 lemon
2 teaspoons soy sauce
¼ pint single cream
salt and pepper

Method

Melt butter and cook onion in a covered saucepan for 15-20 minutes. Add chicken pieces and tarragon and cook for 5 minutes. Stir in the flour and gradually add the stock, lemon rind, lemon juice and soy sauce and cover and cook until the chicken is tender. Allow to cool a little, then stir in cream. This may help the cream not to curdle at this stage. Reheat gently without boiling, season and serve.

Cooking time: 40 minutes

History repeating itself? On the left a postcard from the Alan Barker's collection showing the 1914 rail accident at the Links and on the right a photograph by Mike Drummond of the 1998 derailment at almost the same spot.

Three Bean Soup

Gillian Braid - Burntisland

Ingredients - Serves 8

4 cloves of garlic, crushed
2 tablespoons olive oil
8 oz dried haricot beans, soaked overnight
1 tablespoon tomato purée
3 pints chicken or vegetable stock
8 oz potatoes, diced
8 oz broad beans, thawed if frozen

2 oz small dried pasta, such as vermicelli
20-30 fresh basil leaves, plus a sprig to garnish
salt and ground black pepper
1 lb small French beans, trimmed and halved
8 oz ripe tomatoes
grated fresh Parmesan cheese, to serve

Method

Fry the garlic in the oil for 1 minute. Add the drained haricot beans, tomato purée and stock. Simmer for 15 minutes, then add the potatoes. Simmer for another 15 minutes then add the broad beans, pasta, half the basil and salt and pepper to taste. Simmer for a further 15 minutes. Meanwhile, boil the French beans fast in salted water until just tender. Drain and rinse under cold water to set the colour. Skin the tomatoes, remove the seeds and slice the flesh into long thin strips. Just before serving, add the French beans, raw tomato pieces and the rest of the basil to the soup. Bring back to the boil, pour into bowls and sprinkle with freshly grated Parmesan cheese. Garnish with the basil sprig.

This soup is filling enough to be served as a lunch with plenty of crusty French bread.

Cooking time: 50 minutes

Lettuce, Mint and Pea Soup

Janis Simpson - Burntisland

Ingredients - Serves 4-6

8 oz of lettuce leaves
1 small onion, finely chopped
1 large potato
2 tablespoons fresh mint, finely chopped
¾ pint chicken stock
croutons, to garnish

grated nutmeg
¾ pint milk
4 oz fresh or frozen peas
1½ oz butter
salt and pepper

Method

Thoroughly wash the lettuce leaves and shred them. Melt the butter in a saucepan and fry the onion for 5 minutes until soft. Then add the potato, lettuce, peas and stock. Bring to the boil, then reduce heat. Cover the pan and simmer for 30 minutes. Allow the soup to cool a little, then either rub through a sieve or liquidize the mixture. Return to the pan and add the milk, mint, nutmeg and season to taste with salt and pepper. Reheat gently and serve with the croutons.

Cooking time: 45 minutes

Avocado Surprise

Janet Woods - Ottawa, Canada

Ingredients - Serves 4

2 avocados
6 dried apricots, chopped
5 oz cream cheese
2 oz white Cheshire or white Stilton cheese, grated

5 celery sticks, sliced
salt and freshly ground black pepper
juice of a lemon

Method

Remove avocado flesh. Rub skins with lemon juice. Mix avocado flesh with cream cheese, celery and apricots. Season to taste. Place in the skins. Sprinkle with cheese. Place under a medium high grill and cook until cheese has melted. Serve with walnut bread or crusty rolls as a starter, snack or main course.

Cooking time: 10 minutes

Ham Stuffed Peaches

Jean Muir - Burntisland

Ingredients - Serves 4

1 16 oz can peach halves
4 oz cooked ham, sliced
salt and pepper
parsley sprigs or cress

2 teaspoons chopped parsley or cress
4 tablespoons mayonnaise
lettuce
cherry tomatoes

Method

Strain juice from peaches and drain on kitchen paper. Mince or chop ham finely. Mix the ham with the mayonnaise and parsley. Season to taste. Put mixture into stone cavity of the peaches. Serve on a bed of lettuce with parsley sprigs or cress and cherry tomatoes.

Preparation time: 10 minutes

Pears with Stilton

Tib Simpson - Heritage Trust Volunteer

Ingredients - Serves 4

3 oz Stilton cheese
3 oz cream cheese
4 large ripe dessert pears
lemon juice, for brushing
4 fresh mint sprigs, to garnish

Dressing:

3 tablespoons oil
1 tablespoon lemon juice
1 tablespoon chopped fresh mint
1 teaspoon sugar
salt and black pepper

Method

Beat together the Stilton and cream cheese until soft. Spoon into a piping bag fitted with a large plain nozzle. Meanwhile make the dressing. Put the oil, lemon juice chopped mint, sugar and salt and pepper in a screw top jar. Shake vigorously, then adjust seasoning if necessary. Peel, core and halve each pear. Fan by slicing thinly. Brush with lemon juice to stop browning.

To serve, arrange pear halves on plate by easing into a fan shape. Pipe cream cheese mixture on side of place. Decorate with mint sprig. Spoon mint dressing over the pears and serve.

Preparation time: 10 minutes and chilling

Bakers or Baxters Panel, Burntisland Parish Kirk
Illustration courtesy of John M. Pearson

Can't Cook for Toffee Lentil Soup

Sally Magnusson - Television Presenter

"Wishes Burntisland Heritage all the best. It's a great project and deserves support"

Ingredients - Serves 8

2 pints ham stock (made from stock cubes)
6 oz lentils
1 lb carrots
1 small swede or turnip, chopped
1 large onion, diced

1 stalk of celery, chopped
1 medium potato
salt and pepper
parsley

Method

Place water and stock cubes in a pan and bring to the boil. Wash lentils and place in pan with stock. Simmer for 45 minutes. Peel and wash vegetables. Grate carrot, turnip and potato. Reserve one carrot and cut into cubes. Put all vegetables into stock and cook for a further hour until all the vegetables are cooked through. Garnish with the chopped parsley before serving.

Cooking time: 1 hour 30 minutes

Silberbissen

Jane M. Maltman - Heritage Trust Volunteer

Ingredients - Serves 6

1 large grapefruit
12 oz cream cheese
3 tablespoons sour cream
1 tablespoon chopped onion

1 tablespoon lemon juice
2 tablespoons walnuts
salt and pepper
lettuce, shredded

Method

Mix all the ingredients together, leaving the fruit and nuts till last. Spoon into individual glasses, lined with shredded lettuce and serve with toast or brown bread and butter.
Cooking time: nil

Avocado Stronsay

Chris, Helen and Douglas Robertson - Carnock

Ingredients - Serves 4

1 large, ripe avocado
4 oz smoked salmon trimmings
2 oz Parmesan cheese
¼ pint single cream
lemon juice

Method

Using a Parissiene spoon, ball the avocado and place in lemon juice to stop discolouration. Divide smoked salmon trimmings into four cocotte dishes and then place avocado on top. Pour single cream in cocottes until it just covers the avocado. Sprinkle a thin layer of Parmesan cheese over cream. Place under a hot grill until the cheese has melted and is golden brown. Serve with brown bread and butter. As an alternative to a cocotte dish, a ramekin can be used.
Cooking time: 5 minutes

Stilton Mushrooms

Joyce Higginson - Burntisland Community Award Winner 2000

Ingredients - Serves 4

1 can condensed mushroom soup
2 oz Stilton cheese, crumbled
8 oz button mushrooms, quartered
Garlic bread

Method

Microwave the mushroom soup to warm. Then add the crumbled Stilton cheese, the mushrooms and heat again (do not boil). Stir to combine all the ingredients. Serve with the hot garlic bread.
Cooking time: 15 minutes

Pineapple and Cheese Log

Helen Frier - Heritage Trust Volunteer

Ingredients - Serves 4-6

2 oz gherkins, chopped
4 cherries, chopped
8 oz grated cheese
2 tablespoons mayonnaise

½ onion, grated
½ teaspoon mustard
1 hard-boiled egg, chopped
pineapple for decoration

Method

Mix all the ingredients together and shape into a log. Wrap in tinfoil and leave in fridge to chill for 2 hours. Cut into slices and serve on a bed of lettuce and decorate with pieces of pineapple.
Cooking time: nil

Garlic Mushrooms

Janis Simpson - Burntisland

Ingredients - Serves 4

1lb small button mushrooms
1½ oz butter
2 rashers of streaky bacon thinly sliced
3 cloves of garlic, crushed
1 oz breadcrumbs

2 tablespoons parsley, finely chopped
salt and pepper
1 tablespoon lemon juice
lemon slices to garnish
parsley to garnish

Method

Wipe the mushrooms and cut in half if large. Melt the butter in a pan and fry the mushrooms for 3 minutes until brown. Mix together the bacon, garlic, breadcrumbs, parsley and seasoning. Sprinkle over the mushrooms and cook uncovered over a gentle heat for 10 minutes, stirring the ingredients frequently. Add the lemon juice and adjust the seasoning. Serve immediately, garnished with the lemon wedges and parsley.
Cooking time: 15 minutes

Smoked Mackerel Paté

Ingredients - Serves 4

2 oz butter
2 oz double cream, lightly whipped
8 oz smoked mackerel, skinned and mashed
1 teaspoon of horseradish sauce
lemon juice
salt and pepper to taste

Method

Remove skin and break up the mackerel. Cream butter in a bowl. Add the whipped cream, horseradish sauce, seasoning lemon juice and mackerel. Beat the mixture until smooth. Press the mixture into individual ramekin dishes and chill in the fridge for approximately 1 hour. Garnish with lemon wedges and parsley sprigs. Serve with hot buttered toast.
Preparation time: 20 minutes

Cullen Skink

Alex Salmond MSP

Duncan R. Clark - Headteacher, Burntisland Primary School

Ingredients - Serves 4

2 medium smoked haddock or Finnan haddock or 1 large haddock on the bone
2 medium onions
¾ pint milk
1 lb potatoes, boiled and mashed with a knob of butter
2 oz butter

Method

Put fish in cold water, enough to cover. Bring to the boil and simmer for 10 minutes. Take out fish and remove bones and skin. Flake fish. Cook onion in the butter, taking care not to brown the onion. Add liquid from fish, ¾ pint milk and onion to the mashed potato to form thick creamy soup. Salt, pepper and a small amount of parsley may be added.

Cooking time: 1 hour

Crostini with Smoked Salmon

Kevin Woodford - Celebrity Chef, "Can't Cook Won't Cook"

"Happy cooking!"

Ingredients - Serves 4

1 tablespoon paprika
1 tablespoon chopped fresh dill
4 oz marscapone cheese
3 oz smoked salmon trimmings, finely diced
4 slices of good quality bread, the firmer the better

juice of ¼ lemon
freshly ground black pepper
a pinch cayenne pepper

Method

Mix together the marscapone cheese, smoked salmon, lemon juice, dill and cayenne pepper, adding ground black pepper to taste. Toast the bread on a ridged, cast iron grill pan or fry in a little olive oil until golden brown on both sides. Spread the marscapone and salmon mixture evenly on the toasted bread and heat under the grill just until the topping bubbles. Lightly dust the crostini with the paprika and then serve straight away.

Cooking time: 5 minutes

Egg, Bacon and Parmesan Benedict

Antony Worrall Thompson - Celebrity Chef, "Ready Steady Cook"

"I hope your project is a great success."

Ingredients - Serves 2 as a main course and 4 as a starter

2 hardboiled eggs, peeled and chopped
2 tablespoons chopped flat leaf parsley
4 oz unsalted butter
4 large free-range egg yolks
1 tablespoon snipped chives
1 tablespoon lemon juice
4 oz fatty pancetta or smoked streaky bacon cut into lardons

3 tablespoons grated Parmesan
2 English muffins split in half
4 soft poached eggs (see recipe below)
4 rashers dry cure bacon
salt and ground black pepper

Method

In a heavy frying pan over a low heat, melt the butter. Add the pancetta and cook slowly for about 15-20 minutes until the bacon releases its fats and the meat become slightly crispy. Drain the fat and set aside apart from the meat. Combine the egg yolks with the lemon juice in a double boiler or a bowl over, but not touching simmering water. Beat with a whisk until the yolks thicken. Remove from the heat. Add the bacon fat and butter drop by drop to the egg mix, whisking continually. Keep adding more until all is incorporated and emulsified. Add the crispy bacon meat, the hard-boiled eggs, parsley, chives, Parmesan and seasoning. Keep warm over the boiler, until ready to use. Just before serving, toast the muffins, either pan-fry or grill the bacon rashers until crispy and re-heat the poached eggs by carefully placing them into boiling salted water for 30 seconds and removing them with a slotted spoon. To serve place two bacon rashers on top of a toasted English muffin, top with a warm poached egg and pour over the sauce. Serve immediately.

This is deliciously different, a great topping for Eggs Benedict or Florentine or as a sauce to fold into pasta for a different Carbonara.

Cooking time: 40 minutes

Burntisland Parish Church.
Postcard courtesy of Alan Barker

Burntisland Parish Church was built between 1592 and 1594 in which year it was consecrated. It was the first church to be built in Scotland after the Reformation and is the only one of that period still in use. The proposal to pursue the objective of a new Authorised Version of the Bible was taken at the General Assembly held at the church on 12th May 1601. The now widely used "King James" version of the Bible was the outcome of this proposal. The steps that can be seen in the picture lead to the Sailors Loft. This entrance was provided to allow sailors to enter and leave the church during services without disturbing the rest of the congregation.

Roasted Vegetables on Ciabatta

Phillip Schofield - Actor, TV Presenter

"Good luck with the find."

Ingredients - Serves 2 as main course, 4 as starter

1 red pepper
1 orange pepper
1 red onion
1 yellow courgette
1 green courgette
1 leek

handful chestnut mushrooms
cream cheese
ciabatta loaf
balsamic vinegar (optional)
extra virgin olive oil
salt and pepper

Method

Preheat oven to 190°C/375°F/gas mark 5

I usually use the vegetables listed above but you can use any that need to be eaten (e.g. spring onions, parsnips, carrots etc). Obviously the harder vegetables will need a bit longer to cook. Chop or slice all vegetables and put them all, except the mushrooms, into a large roasting tin. Sprinkle with salt and pepper and drizzle over about 2 tablespoons of olive oil. Roast for about 30-40 minutes in a hot oven until nearly cooked to your liking, then add the mushrooms and roast for a further 10 minutes. While this is cooking, halve the ciabatta length ways and toast the inside under the grill. Spread with a little cream cheese and top with the roasted vegetables. Add seasoning and a little balsamic vinegar to taste.

Cooking time: 40-50 minutes

Thai Hot and Sour Soup

Pam McCaulay - Kirkcaldy

Ingredients - Serves 4

1 tablespoon sunflower oil
8 oz smoked tofu, sliced
3 oz shitake mushrooms sliced
2 tablespoons fresh coriander, chopped
4 oz watercress
1 red chilli, sliced finely, to garnish

Stock:

1 tablespoon tamarind pulp
2 dried red chillies, chopped
2 kaffir lime leaves torn in half
1 inch piece ginger, chopped
2 inch piece galangal, chopped
1 onion, quartered
1¾ pints water

Method

Put all ingredients for the stock into a saucepan and bring to the boil. Simmer for 5 minutes. Remove from the heat and strain, reserving the stock. Heat the oil in a wok or large, heavy frying pan and cook the tofu over a high heat for about 2 minutes, stirring constantly. Add the strained stock. Add the mushrooms and coriander, and boil for 3 minutes. Add the watercress and boil for 1 minute. Serve immediately, garnished with red chillies

Cooking time: 20 minutes

Roasted Tomato and Crab Soup

Paul Rankin - Celebrity Chef, "Ready Steady Cook"

Ingredients - Serves 4-6

1½ ripe plum tomatoes, halved
2 red peppers, seeded and roughly chopped
2 onions, roughly chopped
6 garlic cloves, crushed
3 tablespoons tomato purée
3 tablespoons olive oil
1 teaspoon fresh thyme leaves
2 tablespoons fresh basil leaves
1 tablespoon fresh parsley leaves
salt and freshly ground pepper
water to dilute
sugar

Garnish:

250g crab meat, cooked and cleaned
2 shallots, very finely chopped
1 chilli, finely chopped
2 plum tomatoes, peeled, seeded and diced
1 tablespoon lemon juice
Tabasco sauce (optional)
2 tablespoons chopped coriander leaves
coriander sprigs

Method

Preheat the oven to 200°C/400°F/gas mark 6

In a roasting tin, mix all of the first 6 ingredients. Bake in the hot oven for about an hour, stirring occasionally. The skins of the peppers should blacken slightly. Remove the roasting tray from the oven, and purée the ingredients in a blender. Pass through a sieve. Put the herbs in the blender with some of the soup, and purée for 15 seconds. Adjust the thickness of the soup with water if it is too thick, and season with salt, pepper, and a bit of sugar. Reheat gently in a pan. Mix together in a bowl the shallots, crab, chilli, chopped coriander and lemon juice. Season to taste with salt and pepper. Place a spoonful of the mix in the bottom of each warmed soup plate, and carefully ladle the soup around. Garnish with a sprig of coriander leaf. Serve at once.

Cooking time: 1 hour 15 minutes

Halloumi and Tomato Salad

Janis Simpson - Burntisland

Ingredients - Serves 4

2 large beef tomatoes
2 tablespoons chopped fresh mint
4 oz Halloumi cheese
mint sprigs, to garnish
salt and ground black pepper
8 tablespoons olive oil
flour, for dusting

Method

Slice the tomatoes and arrange them on plates. Sprinkle with 1 tablespoon oil, mint, salt and pepper. Slice the Halloumi cheese thickly and dip the pieces in the flour. Heat the remaining olive oil, shake off the excess flour and fry the cheese on both sides until golden. Drain well on kitchen paper. Arrange the cheese decoratively on the tomatoes. Garnish with mint sprigs and serve while still hot.

Tip: If you have it, use Extra Virgin olive oil for this dish to give the very best flavour.

Cooking time: 5 minutes

Stilton Soup

Sandi Toksvig - TV Personality, "Call My Bluff"

"So you are involved with looking for something buried under four feet of silt. I sympathize as I do that every day in my kitchen looking for a clean coffee cup. Here is a recipe for Stilton soup that is delicious. My cooking skills are based largely on improvisation so I am probably better at making it than telling you about it"

Ingredients - Serves 6

2 "cracking" celery stalks
2 "to make your eyes water" medium onions
1 tablespoon butter (Danish of course)
1 tablespoon flour
8 oz Stilton, *(I don't do metric. It's a sort of big triangle of the stuff. Use less if you don't like such a strong taste).*
4 oz strong cheddar, basically half the amount of Stilton
1½ pints chicken stock (if you're veggie you can use vegetable stock but I don't think it's as good)
3 tablespoons single cream
½ pint milk
2 glasses dry white wine

Method

Chop up the celery and the onion. Fry them in the butter till they are soft but not brown. Add the flour, stir it all up and cook for a minute or two. Add the chicken stock and one glass of the wine, bring just to the boil and then simmer gently for half an hour. Meanwhile crumble the Stilton and grate the chedder.
Drink the other glass of wine.
After half an hour add the cheese and milk. Cook till it is all thoroughly dissolved and mixed in. Take the whole lot and put it through the blender to chop up the onion and celery. (Careful, it's hot!) Put it back in the pan and add the cream. Serve with hot bread. Keep any leftovers, as it tastes even better the next day.
Cooking time: 45 minutes

Special Prawn Cocktail

Cilla Black - TV Personality, "Blind Date"
"Very best wishes for the project."

Ingredients - Serves 4

fresh prawns for four people
melon
cucumber
lemon (optional)

2 tablespoons mayonnaise
1 tablespoon tomato ketchup
dash of Worcestershire sauce or white wine
garlic

Method

To make the sauce mix two tablespoons of mayonnaise with enough tomato ketchup to give it a pale pink colour, mix in a dash of Worcestershire sauce and garlic to taste if desired. To give the sauce a very special taste, substitute dry white wine for the Worcester sauce. Arrange prawns in individual dishes on a bed of lettuce and cucumber. Top with sauce. Cover with cling film and place in refrigerator for 1 hour before serving. Make melon balls with butter scoop or cut half inch squares and add 15 minutes before serving. Replace in refrigerator. Serve with lemon cut into wedges. Alternatively use celery pieces in place of melon.
Preparation time: 1 hour

Cheese, Garlic and Herb Paté

Catherine Truby - Burntisland

Ingredients - Serves 4

6 oz mature cheddar cheese, finely grated
3 spring onions, finely chopped
2 tablespoons chopped, mixed, fresh herbs,
(e.g. parsley, chives, marjoram, oregano and basil)
4-6 slices of white bread from a medium cut sliced loaf
mixed salad leaves and cherry tomatoes

4 oz cream cheese
1 garlic clove, crushed
pepper
½ oz butter

To garnish:
ground paprika
sprigs of fresh herbs

Method

Melt the butter in a small frying pan. Fry the garlic and spring onions together gently for 3-4 minutes, until softened. Allow to cool. Put the cream cheese into a large mixing bowl and beat until soft. Add the garlic and spring onions. Stir in the herbs, mixing well. Add the cheddar cheese and work the mixture together to form a stiff paste. Cover and chill until ready to serve. To make the Melba toast, toast the slices of bread on both sides, and then cut off the crusts. Using a sharp bread knife cut through the bread horizontally to make very thin slices. Cut into triangles and then grill the untoasted sides lightly. Arrange the mixed salad leaves on 4 serving plates with the cherry tomatoes. Pile the cheese on top and sprinkle with a little paprika. Garnish with sprigs of fresh herbs and serve with the melba toast.

Preparation time: 35 minutes

The Porte and entrance gates to The Links
Postcard courtesy of Joyce Higginson

Oliver Cromwell's troops captured the town after the Battle of Inverkeithing in 1651. In 1654 Cromwell's troops, who were garrisoned at Burntisland, held a horse race from the Links to Pettycur Sands with a silver cup as a prize. That race is considered to be the start of the Highland Games, which continue to this day.
The Links is common ground and has been used for bleaching linen, grazing cattle, playing golf and for holding the annual market and fair.

Real Tomato Soup

Rt. Hon. Gordon Brown MP - Chancellor of the Exchequer, North Queensferry

"I wish you well with your fundraising"

Ingredients - Serves 6

2 lb of fresh tomatoes
1 potato, peeled and cut into small chunks
2 tablespoons of olive oil
2 cloves of garlic
1 teaspoon of sugar
salt and pepper
½ pint of water
bowls and spoons for serving

Garnish:

fromage frais (lower in calories than cream)
a little chopped parsley or basil
Utensils:
large roasting tin
saucepan
blender, food processor, or a sieve

Method

Preheat oven to 190ºC/375ºF/gas mark 5

Nothing beats "real" tomato soup at any time of the year. It is also really easy to make.

Add half the oil to the roasting tin to cover the base. Cut all the tomatoes in half and place in the bottom of the tin along with the peeled garlic, pour the remainder of the oil over the tomatoes and season with salt and pepper. Bake in the oven for 30 minutes.

Put potatoes in a saucepan along with the water and boil for 15 minutes until they are soft. Remove the potatoes but reserve the water from the pan as this is used as the stock for the soup.

Take the tomatoes from the oven and remove the skins with a fork. Place tomatoes, potatoes, garlic and water in a liquidiser or blender and blend until smooth.

Return the soup to the saucepan and heat through (if soup is too thick, add a little more water). The soup is now ready to serve. Ladle into bowls and add a spoon of fromage frais, sprinkle with chopped parsley and serve with crusty bread.

Cooking time: 40 minutes

Spicy Lemon Grass Soup

Thalia Teasdale - Portsmouth

Ingredients - Serves 4

150g mushrooms
4 stalks fresh lemon grass
2 fresh red chillies
60ml lemon juice
½ teaspoon chilli paste
150g prawns
30ml fish sauce
800ml fish stock (chicken or vegetable can be used)

Method

Chop mushrooms, lemon grass and red chillies. Heat stock in a saucepan and add the chopped vegetables. Add all the other ingredients and allow to simmer for 5 to 10 minutes until the vegetables are tender. Serve with crusty bread.

Preparation time: 15 minutes
Cooking time: 10 minutes

MAIN COURSES

<u>Why Asking Hubby To Help With The Shopping
Isn't Always A Good Idea.</u>

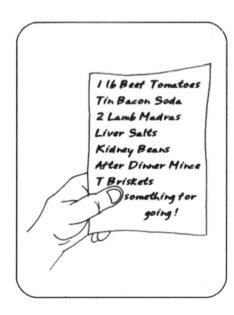

Smoked Salmon and Asparagus Pasta Sauce

Gillian Braid - Burntisland

Ingredients - Serves 6

4 oz low fat cheese
6 oz smoked salmon trimmings, chopped
4 tablespoons dry white wine
1 teaspoon lemon juice

1 tablespoon chopped dill
12 oz asparagus trimmed and cut into 2 inch pieces
8 oz tagliatelle

Method

Put cheese, 2 oz salmon, wine and lemon juice into a food processor and chop until smooth. Transfer to a saucepan and heat gently (do not boil). Season with salt and pepper, stir in chopped dill. Cook asparagus lightly in salted boiling water for 5 minutes until just tender and drain. Cook pasta until *al dente*, drain and return to saucepan. Add the sauce, asparagus and the rest of the smoked salmon trimmings, carefully toss in the pasta and serve immediately.

Cooking time: 40 minutes

Braised Beef in Walnut, Chilli, and Chocolate Sauce

Lesley Braid - Burntisland

Ingredients - Serves 4

1 rounded tablespoon cocoa powder
1½ lb braising beef, cubed
1 pint beef stock
1 bunch spring onions
1 teaspoon cinnamon
3 tablespoons oil
14 oz can chopped tomatoes

3 oz finely ground walnuts
1 medium onion, roughly chopped
3-4 chillies, de-seeded and chopped
1 large clove garlic, chopped
1 oz raisins
4-5 whole cloves

Method

Preheat oven at 150°C/300°F/gas mark 2.

Put first 8 ingredients in food processor and blend until smooth. Heat 2 tablespoon of oil in a pan, add cinnamon and stir, then add processed mixture and let it cook gently stirring constantly for 5 minutes.

Now stir in stock, remove pan from heat and add salt to taste. Place 1 tablespoon of oil in a pan and bring to a very high heat and brown the meat then place in a casserole dish, add sauce and any meat juices. Cover and cook in oven for 2½ -3 hours. Before serving stir in the spring onions.

Cooking time: 3 hours

Greek Moussaka

Isa Duncanson - Burntisland Community Award Winner 1981

Ingredients - Serves 4

3 tablespoons oil
1 small onion, chopped
1 lb cooked minced lamb
2¼ oz can tomato purée
salt and pepper
½ lb raw potatoes, sliced
sprig of parsley

1 large aubergine, sliced
1 clove of garlic, crushed
½ lb peeled and sliced tomatoes
½ pint cheese sauce
2 oz grated cheese
1 egg yolk

Method

Preheat oven to 190°C/375°F/gas mark 5

In frying pan, gently fry onion, add minced lamb and shake over heat for 4 minutes. Remove from heat; add tomato purée and season. Put in ovenproof dish and keep warm. Fry potato slices till brown and place on top of the meat. Fry aubergine for 5-7 minutes. Add garlic and sliced tomatoes, cook for a further 5 minutes, pour over potatoes. Prepare cheese sauce and add the egg yolk. Pour over dish and sprinkle with cheese. Bake in a moderate oven for 15-20 minutes. Garnish with parsley.

Cooking time: 40 minutes

Pork in Mushroom Sauce

Cathie O'Harrow - Burntisland Community Award Winner 1991

Ingredients - Serves 4

4 pieces pork fillet
1 oz flour
salt and pepper
2 oz butter
4 oz button mushrooms, thinly sliced
1 16 oz tin carrots, drained and diced
¼ pint double cream
1 tablespoon chopped chives

Method

Beat out the pork and coat in flour, season with salt and pepper. Fry in butter for 3-4 minutes, then stir in the remaining flour and cook for a further minute. Remove from heat, add half carrots and stir in the cream. Reheat gently. Do not boil. Pour over pork and garnish with remaining carrots and chives.

Cooking time: 15 minutes

Malaysian Chicken

Margaret Barclay - Cowdenbeath

Ingredients - Serves 4

4 chicken fillets
1 oz seasoned flour
1 oz butter
1 lb small new potatoes
1 large onion chopped
1 teaspoon ground ginger

2 tablespoons clear honey
1 15 oz can crushed pineapple
1 oz cornflour
½ pint chicken stock
salt and pepper

Method

Preheat oven to 180°C/350°F/gas mark 4

Toss chicken fillets in flour and fry in butter till lightly browned, transfer to a shallow ovenproof dish. Arrange the potatoes between the chicken pieces. Fry the onion in butter until transparent, stir in ginger, honey and pineapple. Blend cornflour with stock and add to the onion mixture. Adjust seasoning, bring back to the boil and pour sauce over chicken. Cover and bake at for 1 hour.

Cooking time: 1 hour

Chilli Con Carne

Dr. Lewis Moonie MP - Defence Minister, Kirkcaldy

"I wish you well in your fund raising efforts."

Ingredients - Serves 8

2 lb finely diced lean steak (rump)
1 onion, finely chopped
1 large clove garlic, crushed
2 1 lb tins red kidney beans, drained and rinsed
chilli powder to taste - as hot as you wish
salt and pepper

2 tablespoons oil
2 tins chopped tomatoes
1 pkt passata

Method

Fry onion, garlic and beef in oil until brown. Add tomatoes, passata and chilli powder. Simmer for one hour then add the beans; simmer with lid off until most of the liquid has evaporated. Season with salt and pepper as required.
Serve with tortillas, salad and lots of beer!
Cooking time: 45 minutes

Pan Haggerty

Agnes McGregor - Kirkcaldy

Ingredients - Serves 6

2 lb potatoes
1 lb onions, peeled and sliced
8 oz chipolata sausages, sliced

4 oz grated cheddar cheese
salt and pepper

Method

Peel, slice and boil potatoes. Place with onions in a well-greased frying pan in layers. Season well. Finish with sliced chipolata sausages and cheese. Cover pan with lid. Cook for about 20-30 minutes or until potatoes are soft. Place under grill until the grated cheese begins to bubble, then serve immediately.
Cooking time: 45 minutes

Potted Hough - I

Agnes McGregor - Kirkcaldy

Ingredients - Serves 6-8

2-2½ lb Hough
1 ox tail

1 knapp bone (knuckle)
2 Oxo cubes

Method

Place hough, ox tail and knapp bone in pot, cover with water and bring to the boil. Simmer gently for 2- 2½ hours or until the bones start to break up. Remove from pot. Take out all the fat and bones and chop meat up. Replace in pot and bring to the boil again. Mix 2 Oxo cubes in a little hot water and add. Simmer for ten minutes. Add salt and black pepper to season. Pour into bowls. When cool, place in fridge to set.
Cooking time: 3 hours

Crusty Shepherds Pie

Kathie O'Harrow - Kirkcaldy

Ingredients - Serves 4

1 tablespoon olive oil
14 oz passata
1 onion, chopped
1 lb minced lamb
1 teaspoon dried oregano
2 tablespoons chopped parsley
½ pint red wine
4 rashers smoked streaky bacon, chopped

Scone topping:

8 oz self-raising flour
2 oz chilled butter diced
2 teaspoons whole grain mustard
3 oz mature cheddar cheese, grated
4 fl oz milk
salt and pepper

Method

Preheat oven to 200ºC/400ºF/gas mark 6

Heat oil in pan, add bacon and onion fry for 5 minutes. Add the lamb and fry, stirring until evenly browned. Stir in the herbs, wine and passata and season. Bring to the boil then lower heat and simmer uncovered for 25 minutes until lamb is tender and sauce has thickened.

Put flour in a bowl; add salt and pepper to taste. Rub in diced butter until mixture resembles bread-crumbs. Stir in the mustard and 2 oz of the cheese, and then add enough milk to make soft dough.

Knead dough lightly on a floured surface then roll out to ½ inch thickness. Cut into 2 inch scone shapes. Transfer the meat mixture into a greased 2 pint casserole or pie dish and arrange the scones on top of the mixture. Brush with milk and sprinkle the remaining cheese over the surface of the scones. Bake in a preheated oven for 25 minutes until the topping is golden brown.

Cooking time: 1 hour

The Binn Village
Postcard courtesy of Alan Barker

The Binn Village lay east of Burntisland and was built to accommodate Binnend Oil Company employees and their families. Inaugurated in 1878, this company produced shale oil and by-products until it was devastated by fire 1892. The works was finally shut down in 1905. Following closure, the cottages provided cheap lodgings for holidaymakers from Edinburgh.

Beef Goulash, Mashed Potato and Caramelised Red Cabbage

Kelly Cooper Barr - Socialite and Fashion Stylist, Glasgow

Ingredients - Serves 6

2½ lb lean, diced stewing beef
2 tablespoons oil
2 Spanish onions
3 cloves of garlic, crushed
2 heaped teaspoons paprika
1 heaped teaspoon cayenne pepper
2 oz flour
3 pints beef stock
300g tomato purée

Cabbage:
1 red cabbage
4 apples peeled, cored and sliced
1 bottle of red wine
4 heaped teaspoons of brown sugar
1 cup of raisins
Potatoes:
2 lb potatoes
butter and cream
olive oil
salt and pepper

Method

Brown the meat, and remove from the pan. Add the onion, garlic, paprika, cayenne, and fry for 3 minutes. Stir in the flour and cook for 2 minutes. Remove pan from the heat and gradually add the beef stock. Add meat to pan along with tomato purée. Return to heat, and bring to the boil stirring continuously. Season to taste, and simmer for 2 hours.

Mashed potato:
Peel and boil potatoes. When cooked add butter and cream; add a little olive oil. Mash, then cream with an electric mixer for extra fluffiness.

Caramelised red cabbage:
Shred cabbage and place all ingredients in a pan and simmer until all liquid has evaporated and cabbage is cooked. Care must be taken that this does not burn. Serve with sour cream or crème fraîche and finely sliced spring onion.

Cooking time: 2 hours

Bobotie

Lyn Wolfendale - Godalming

Ingredients - Serves 6

1 cup milk
1 thick slice of white bread
1 tablespoon olive oil
12 almonds, blanched and roughly chopped
2¼ lb ground beef
2 teaspoons apricot jam
¼ cup lemon juice
½ cup seedless raisins

10 dried apricots
2 tablespoons mild curry powder
1 large onion chopped
1 teaspoon salt
freshly ground black pepper
6 bay leaves
2 eggs

Method

Preheat oven to 180°C/350°F/gas mark 4

Put half the milk in a shallow dish, add bread and soak for 5 minutes. Heat oil in a flameproof casserole dish. Add onion and cook, stirring occasionally for 5 minutes or until soft. Squeeze milk from bread and add to dish with all remaining ingredients except eggs and remaining milk. Mix well then level surface. Bake 30 minutes. Beat together the remaining milk and eggs and pour over meat.

Return to the oven and bake for a further 20-25 minutes or until the custard is set.

Cooking time: 30 minutes

Crunchy Chicken Fillets, Stuffed with Haggis, in a Creamy Tarragon Sauce.

Susan Madley - Delicate Essence, Burntisland

Ingredients - Serves 2

2 large chicken fillets
4 oz haggis
4 fl oz double cream
4 oz porridge oats
salt and pepper
3 tablespoons dried tarragon
4 oz crème fraîche
1 egg beaten
olive oil
fresh tarragon to garnish

Method

Using a sharp knife enlarge the slit in the back of the chicken fillets to create a pocket.
Roll the haggis into two sausages, just shorter than the chicken fillets. Stuff the fillets with the haggis and chill in the fridge for 10 minutes to firm. Place the porridge oats, salt pepper and one tablespoon of the dried tarragon into a polythene bag and shake to mix ingredients. Remove fillets from fridge and dip in egg. Place in bag and shake, ensuring that both fillets are well coated. Place one inch of olive oil in a pan and heat. When oil is medium hot add the chicken to the pan and fry gently for 20-25 minutes ensuring that the chicken is cooked through. Remove and keep warm. Put cream, crème fraîche and the remaining tarragon into a heavy-based pan and boil to reduce. To serve pour sauce onto plates, place chicken on top and garnish with fresh tarragon. Serve with new potatoes and steamed broccoli.
Cooking time: 25 minutes

Brazilian Cod with Coconut

Hazel Simpson - Heritage Trust Volunteer

Ingredients - Serves 6

2 tablespoons olive oil
1 large Spanish onions, finely sliced
4 spring onions, trimmed and chopped
2 cloves garlic, crushed
1 green chilli, seeded and finely chopped
1 green pepper, sliced
14 oz tin chopped tomatoes

3 tablespoons finely chopped fresh parsley
1 tablespoon fresh coriander, finely chopped
salt and black pepper
12 fl oz coconut milk
1½ lb skinned cod fillets
boiled rice to serve

Method

Heat the oil in a large flameproof casserole dish. Gently fry the sliced onion. Add the spring onions, garlic cloves, chilli and the green pepper. Cook for 2 minutes. Add the tomatoes and cook for 5 minutes. Stir in the parsley and coriander. Season to taste with salt and pepper. Pour over enough coconut milk to make a thick sauce. Stir. Gently bring to the boil, then reduce the heat and stir again. Add the fish fillets and simmer for 15 minutes. Season to taste. Serve immediately on the rice.
Cooking time: 30 minutes

Harrira (Moroccan Chickpea Broth)

Hamish Brown - Climber and Author, Burntisland

Ingredients - Serves 14

2 400g tins chickpeas
1 400g tin chickpea Dahl
1 cup lentils or split peas
2-3 cups rice
2 cups of any small pasta
3 onions, diced
2 large carrots, diced
½ small swede turnip, diced
50 g tomato purée
2 large tomatoes, diced
2 tablespoons vegetable oil

100 g minced mutton or lamb
if vegetarian use vegetable stock
1 teaspoon cumin
2 pinches saffron
½ teaspoon salt
2 teaspoons fresh ground black pepper
juice of ½ a lemon
2 eggs, beaten
7 pints water
1 bunch fresh coriander

Method

A large pan is required for this recipe, if a smaller quantity is desired, halve the ingredients.
Fry meat in a pan with the oil to seal, add the water to the pan and bring to the boil. Add the rice, lentils and diced vegetables. Cook for 1 hour. Once the pulses start to soften add the rest of the ingredients except the eggs, starting with the pasta. Simmer for a further 30 minutes until the soup is cooked, add the two beaten eggs into the hot soup and stir well.
This dish is eaten after fasting for Ramadan and is almost a meal in itself.
Cooking time: 1 hour 30 minutes

Decompression Chilli

Carl Galfskiy - Heritage Trustee and Diver

Ingredients - Serves 4

½ kilo of minced lamb
1 medium tin of skinned plum tomatoes
1 small tin of kidney beans, drained and rinsed
1 large red onion, chopped
2 large fresh tomatoes, chopped
50 g tomato purée
1 clove garlic
¼ teaspoon chilli powder

4 large mushrooms, sliced
250 ml of tomato ketchup
50 ml sweet chilli sauce or golden syrup
12 small hot red peppers, finely chopped
½ teaspoon curry powder
7 tablespoons water
4 tablespoons oil for frying

Method

Brown mince and onions in a pan on a high heat with the oil. Add the tinned tomatoes, red peppers, kidney beans, fresh tomatoes, tomato purée, garlic, chilli powder, curry powder and mushrooms. Stir well. Now add the ketchup, chilli sauce and water, simmer for 30 minutes. Stir and add more water if necessary and cook for a further 30 minutes. Serve with rice or buttered toast.
Cooking time: 1 hour

WARNING: It should be noted that any diver who eats this dish within two hours prior to diving may experience buoyancy control problems throughout the dive. On surfacing, it is essential that either an extremely friendly boatman, or a friend with a cold or no sense of smell, is on hand to open the zips of the dry-suit of the diver in question.

Sweet and Sour Chicken

Stephen Hendry - World Champion Snooker Player

Ingredients - Serves 4

4 chicken portions
salt and freshly ground black pepper
30 ml dripping or oil
200g tin pineapple rings
30 ml soy sauce
15 ml tomato ketchup
15 ml wine vinegar

15 ml soft brown sugar
1 onion, peeled and sliced
1 red or green pepper, cored, seeded and sliced
15 ml plain flour
425 g tin tomatoes
freshly boiled rice to serve

Method

Preheat the oven to 180°C/350°F/gas mark 4

Season chicken portions all over with salt and pepper. Heat the dripping or oil in a frying pan, add the chicken and fry until well browned all over. Transfer to a casserole dish. Drain the pineapple, reserving the syrup; chop two rings and sprinkle over the chicken. Reserve the remaining pineapple for the garnish. Make up the syrup to ¼ pint with water. Add the soy sauce, ketchup, vinegar and sugar to the syrup. Add the onion and red or green pepper to the frying pan and fry in the same fat until tender. Stir in the flour and cook for 1 minute, then add the pineapple syrup mixture and tomatoes and bring to the boil, stirring well. Add salt and pepper to taste and simmer for 2 minutes. Pour over the chicken, cover the casserole and cook in a preheated oven for about 45 minutes or until the chicken is tender. Serve with freshly boiled rice and garnish each piece of chicken with half a pineapple ring.

Cooking time: 1 hour

War Memorial, Burntisland
Postcard courtesy of Alan Barker

The comemorative plaques for the second world war are mounted on a stone enclosur which replaces the fence shown in the picture.
Books of Remembrance from the First and
Second World Wars can be viewed by arrangement.

Akee and Saltfish (served with Cornmeal Muffins)

Ainsley Harriot - Celebrity Chef, "Can't Cook Won't Cook"

Ingredients - Serves 6

1 1b salted cod
splash of lemon juice
1 large tin of akees, drained and lightly rinsed
1 red pepper, seeded and sliced
1 green pepper, seeded and sliced
1 small chilli, seeded and sliced (optional)
2 tomatoes skinned and chopped
1 tablespoon fresh chopped parsley

3 spring onions, sliced at an angle
1 small onion, finely sliced
1 sprig of fresh thyme or:
¼ teaspoon dried thyme
2-4 tablespoons corn oil
freshly ground black pepper
3 hard boiled eggs

Method

Soak the fish overnight or for at least 2-3 hours to remove saltiness. Drain and put into a saucepan covered with water and lemon juice. Bring to the boil and simmer for 15-20 minutes, until tender. Drain and remove skin and bones. Flake the fish and put to one side.

In the corn oil, gently fry the onion, peppers, spring onion and thyme for 3-4 minutes, stirring occasionally.

Then add the chilli, tomatoes, and flaked fish and lightly fold in the akees. Heat gently for 8-10 minutes and season with freshly ground black pepper. Garnish with wedges of hard-boiled eggs, sprinkle with chopped parsley and serve with hot cornmeal muffins.

Muffins

Ingredients

8 oz self-raising flour
4 oz fine cornmeal
1½ teaspoons baking powder
1 beaten egg

pinch of salt
3 oz melted butter
5-6 fl oz milk

Method

Preheat oven to 190°C/375°F/gas mark 5

Sift the flour, cornmeal, baking powder and salt into a bowl. Make a well in the middle and add egg and ¾ of the milk. Mix well then add the melted butter and mix until soft but firm. If it is too firm add a little more milk. Butter your muffin tins well and drop a spoonful of the mixture in each cup. This mixture should make about twelve muffins. Bake for 15-20 min until golden brown.

Cooking time: 1 hour

Chinese Style Steak

Cilla Black - TV Personality, "Blind Date"

Ingredients - Serves 4

4 fillet or sirloin steaks
black peppercorns
2 oz butter
2 tablespoons oil

4 oz mushrooms
cream
soy sauce

Method

Crush the black peppercorns in a pestle and mortar and press them into the steak. Leave for at least twenty minutes to allow the flavour to penetrate. Melt some butter in a frying pan (add a touch of oil to stop the butter burning) then add the steaks.

Throw in some finely sliced mushrooms then stir them round the steak while it cooks. When the steak is ready, add some cream and enough soy sauce to colour, and taste is right. It should be a light brown. Serve the steak with the sauce and garnish with vegetables or a salad.

Cooking time: 10-15 minutes

Muscat-Baked Almond Chicken (Lebanese)

Ingredients - Serves 6

4½ lb free range chicken
salt and freshly ground black pepper
½ teaspoon cinnamon
large pinch of nutmeg
fresh lemon thyme
fresh marjoram
8 oz Muscat grapes, skinned, seeded and halved

8 fl oz sweet Muscat wine
½ oz butter
3 tablespoons sliced blanched almonds
2 oz ground almonds
¼ pint single cream
2 egg yolks

Method

Preheat the oven to 200°C/400°F/gas mark 6

Wash the chicken and pat dry with absorbent kitchen paper. Rub it all over with cinnamon, nutmeg, salt and pepper. Take 2-3 sprigs of lemon thyme and the marjoram and put them inside the chicken.

Place it in a casserole and stuff with half the grapes and pour over the wine. Cover and cook in the oven for 1½ hours.

Remove the chicken from the oven and transfer it to a warm serving dish. Remove the grapes and herbs from the cavity. Joint the chicken and cover it with foil to keep it warm. In a small saucepan, melt the butter and sauté the sliced almonds for a few minutes until just coloured. Remove with a slotted spoon and set aside. Skim the fat from the chicken cooking juices in the casserole and strain into the saucepan. Heat the juices gently until very hot, but not boiling, and stir it in the remaining grapes and the ground almonds. Allow to cook for a few minutes to combine the flavours.

In a small bowl, beat the cream and egg yolks together lightly. Take a spoonful of the hot chicken stock and stir it into the egg. Remove the saucepan from the heat and stir in the egg mixture; the sauce should thicken as you stir. Pour some of the sauce over the jointed chicken and sprinkle it with the toasted almonds. Pour the remainder into a sauceboat. **Cooking time: 2 hours**

Fillets of Halibut with a Cheese and Mustard Glaze

Christopher Trotter - Scotland's Larder

Ingredients - Serves 4

4-6 oz halibut steaks
7 oz grated Tobermory Cheddar
3 teaspoons whole grain mustard

double cream
salt and pepper

Method

Butter the base of an ovenproof dish. Place the fish skin side down in the dish. Season with salt and pepper. Mix the grated cheese and mustard together, with enough cream to form a spreadable but thick paste. Season with salt and pepper. Spread the mixture evenly over the fish. Bake in a hot oven 200°C/400°F/gas mark 6 for 20 minutes. The top will be browned and bubbling with the lovely flaky fish underneath. **Cooking time: 20 minutes**

Prawn and Vegetable Stir Fry

Jeanne Rankin - Celebrity Chef, "Ready Steady Cook"

Ingredients - Serves 4

6 oz frozen, cooked, peeled prawns
½ tablespoon corn oil
¼ teaspoon, onion seeds
4-6 curry leaves
4 oz frozen peas
4 oz frozen sweet corn
1 large courgette, sliced

1 medium red pepper de-seeded and chopped
1 teaspoon of crushed coriander seeds
1 teaspoon of crushed, dried red chillies
1 tablespoon of lemon juice
1 tablespoon of fresh coriander leaves, to garnish
salt

Method

Thaw the prawns and drain them of any excess liquid. Heat the oil with the onion seeds and curry leaves in a non-stick wok or frying pan. Add the prawns to the wok and stir-fry until the liquid has evaporated. Next add the peas, sweetcorn, courgette and red pepper. Continue to stir-fry for 3-5 minutes.
Finally, add the coriander seeds, chillies, salt to taste and lemon juice. Serve immediately, garnished with fresh coriander leaves.

Cooking time: 15 minutes

Eezy Peezy Pizza

Lorraine Kelly - TV Presenter - GMTV

Ingredients - Serves 4

For the topping:

14 oz tin chopped tomatoes
1 onion, finely chopped
1 teaspoon chilli powder
(or) a jar of ready-made tomato sauce
1 tablespoon tomato purée
3 large red peppers cut into thick strips
12 pitted olives (optional)

3 tablespoons olive oil
8 oz large flat mushrooms, sliced
1½ tablespoons dried basil
3 oz chopped almonds or any nuts
2 oz Parmesan cheese
2 oz Cheddar cheese, grated
salt and pepper

For the base:

1 10oz packet pizza dough mix
or 4 3oz ready made pizza bases

Method

Preheat the oven to 200°C/400°F/gas mark 6
Making pizza has never been easier. Here's how to transform ready-made pizza bases into something spectacular. Make up the pizza bases according to the instructions on the packet and place on a greased baking tray. Simmer the tomatoes, tomato purée, onion and chilli powder together in a saucepan for 8-10 minutes until thick and reduced. Spread tomato mixture over the pizza base (or, if using ready made tomato sauce, spread sauce from jar over pizza base). Scatter over the peppers and mushrooms and season well with salt and pepper. Sprinkle over the dried basil, the almonds (or nuts) and the Parmesan. Scatter over the Cheddar cheese and olives. Drizzle over 3 tablespoons of olive oil and bake for 15-20 minutes or until bubbling hot and golden brown. Serve at once.

Cooking time: 15-20 minutes

Burntisland Golf Club
Postcard courtesy of Alan Barker

It is known that a form of golf was played on the "Links" at Burntisland as early as 1660. But it was not until the late 18th century that a golf club was formed. Burntisland Old Club is rated as 10th oldest in Britain, founded in 1797.

Lamb's Liver with Ginger and Coriander (Vietnamese)
Pam McCaulay - Kirkcaldy

Ingredients - Serves 4

1 lb lamb's liver cut into 1½ inch wide strips and cut again crosswise into strips, ½ inch thick
½ tablespoon vegetable oil
1 large onion, cut into wedges about 1½ inches wide
2 medium sweet green peppers, halved
1 tablespoon sesame oil
salt

Sauce:

2 tablespoons Nuoc Mam sauce or light soy sauce
2 tablespoons rice wine or dry sherry
2 teaspoons sugar
2 large cloves garlic, coarsely chopped
1 tablespoon fermented black beans, rinsed and coarsely chopped
2 1inch slices root ginger, peeled and minced
1 tablespoon fresh coriander, chopped
1 spring onion, coarsely chopped
2 teaspoons cornflour mixed with 2 tablespoons water

Method

Bring a large saucepan half full of water to the boil. Put in the liver slices and stir until the water begins to bubble into a boil again. Drain the liver and hold under the cold tap to stop the cooking. Drain and set aside. Combine the Nuoc Mam sauce, rice wine and sugar and stir until the sugar dissolves. Heat a wok over high heat and add 1 tablespoon oil. Scatter in the onions and peppers and stir and toss vigorously until they are shining. Sprinkle in some salt and stir for about 1 minute until the onions are translucent. Transfer to a dish. Wipe the wok, add the remaining oil and put in the garlic, black beans, ginger, coriander and spring onions and stir for about 30 seconds to sear them. Add the liver slices to the wok and stir for a further 30 seconds. Add the Nuoc Mam mixture and toss the meat.

Add the cooked vegetables and stir them around so they integrate with the meat. Add the cornflour to the wok, a little at a time, stirring constantly. Sprinkle in the sesame oil, toss a couple of times, and ladle out on a hot serving dish. **Cooking time: 15 minutes**

Trout with Almonds

Jimmy Logan - Scottish Comedian

"It is not generally known that an ancestor of mine HISBISCUS TRIUS LOGAN was in charge of the entertainment on the "Blessing of Burntisland". He lost a case of musical bells so if you find them you can let me know."

Ingredients - Serves 2

2 rainbow trout
salt and pepper
1 oz butter
juice of a lemon
toasted almond slices

4 tablespoons water
4 fl oz double cream
1 tablespoon chives
1 tablespoon Brandy

Method

Preheat oven to 180°C/350°F/gas mark 4

See that the trout are cleaned and season the insides with salt and pepper. Add a lump of butter to the inside. Place in a baking dish and add juice of a lemon and 4 tablespoons of water. Place in the oven and cook for 10-12 minutes.

In a small saucepan add double cream and chives and bring it through the boil. Add a little brandy (if you wish).

Take the trout out of the oven and pour over the cream and chive sauce, making sure that all the fish is covered. Add sliced almonds and place under the grill. When the almonds turn brown take out from under the grill. Serve with mashed potatoes as they absorb the juices.

Cooking time: 20 minutes

Roast Loin of Scotch Pork with Sausage, Apricot and Raisin Stuffing

David S. Wilson - Peat Inn, by Cupar

"Best wishes with the project"

Ingredients - Serves 8

4 lb boneless loin of pork
1 large onion, finely chopped
12 oz pork sausage-meat
8 oz dried apricots, diced
4 oz dried raisins
grated zest of 2 oranges
2 tablespoons flat leaf parsley, chopped

1 teaspoon fresh thyme leaves
1 teaspoon fresh oregano leaves
½ teaspoon freshly ground black pepper
3 cloves garlic minced
½ teaspoon salt
2 tablespoons olive oil

Method

Preheat oven to 180°C/350°F/gas mark 4

Heat oil in frying pan add chopped onion, sweat until soft then add pork sausage-meat. Cook with onions until browned, transfer to large bowl. Add apricots, raisins, herbs, garlic, orange zest, salt and pepper mix well. Fill the pocket in centre of loin with this mixture. Roll long edges around stuffing, tie then place on rack in shallow roasting tin. Place tin on middle shelf of oven cook for 45 minutes, basting occasionally.

Add cup of veal stock to pan, continue to roast and baste for a further 45 minutes, until internal temperature reads 150°F or until the juices run clear. Remove from oven and allow to rest for 15 minutes. Serve with roasting juices.

Cooking time: 1 hour 30 minutes

Pasta with Broccoli

Loyd Grossman - TV Personality, "Master Chef"

Ingredients - Serves as many as you would like

turnip greens or purple broccoli
olive oil
1 tin anchovies
Parmesan cheese grated (optional)

2-3 cloves garlic
2 crushed chilli peppers
pasta (orrechiette, fusilli or penne)

Method

This recipe is a great standby based on a dish from Southern Italy that uses turnip greens. Broccoli is easier to find in Britain and this is best made with purple sprouting broccoli rather than the indestructible, and pretty tasteless, Calabrese type that is in our markets year round.

Finely chop a few cloves of garlic and soften them in a little (about two tablespoons) of olive oil over a very low flame. When the garlic just begins to colour, add two crushed dried chilli peppers. Cook for a further few minutes. Then add one tin of anchovies and continue cooking until the anchovies break up and mix into the sauce. Add as much cooked (steamed, boiled or microwaved) broccoli as you like, a cupful should do. At this point you may wish to add a little more olive oil.

Meanwhile boil your choice of pasta. The classic shape to use is orrechiete but this also works well with fusilli or penne. Drain the cooked pasta, put it into the pan full of sauce and mix gently until the pasta is coated. Strictly speaking you shouldn't serve this dish with grated Parmesan, but I do.

Cooking time: 40 minutes

Deep Fried Crispy Fingers of Pork

Lyn Wolfendale - Godalming

Ingredients - Serves 5-6

½ lb lean pork
1 teaspoon salt
½ teaspoon pepper
½ teaspoon ground ginger
1 tablespoon rice wine or dry sherry
1 teaspoon sesame seed oil
vegetable oil for deep-frying

Batter:
1 egg
1¼ oz plain flour
¾ oz cornflour

Sauce:

1½ tablespoon vegetable oil
1½ tablespoon spring onion, chopped
2 teaspoons garlic, crushed
2 teaspoons fresh chilli, chopped
1½ tablespoons fresh root ginger, chopped
5 tablespoons good stock
2 tablespoons vinegar
2 tablespoons light soy sauce
1 teaspoon salt
1 teaspoon sugar

Method

To make the dip sauce, heat the oil in a wok or pan. When hot, add the onion, garlic, chilli and ginger and stir for a few seconds. Add the rest of the dip sauce ingredients. Bring to the boil, and then pour into a small heatproof bowl

To make the batter, mix the egg, flour and cornflour together.

Cut the pork into finger sized strips. Mix the salt, pepper, ginger, wine or sherry and sesame oil together. Add the pork and mix thoroughly. Leave to marinate for 10 minutes.

Heat the oil in a wok or deep fryer. When very hot, dip the pork fingers in the batter and put gently into the oil. Fry for about 3 minutes then drain. Allow the oil to reheat, then fry the pork again for 30 seconds. Drain again. Arrange the pork fingers on a heated plate and serve with the dip sauce.

Cooking time: 30 minutes

Marinated Spicy Langoustine with Noodles

Nick Nairn - Celebrity Chef. "Ready Steady Cook"

"Good luck with your fund raising efforts."

Ingredients - Serves 4

Langoustine:
20 large langoustine
1 tablespoon light soy sauce
1 tablespoon Nam Plas (Thai fish sauce)
1 red chilli, de-seeded and very finely chopped
juice and zest from 1 lime
4 fl oz olive oil
2 teaspoons fresh coriander, chopped

Noodles:
4 oz quick cook noodles
2 teaspoons sesame oil
4 spring onions, finely chopped
2 tablespoons fresh coriander, chopped

Method

For the marinade, mix all the ingredients together in a small mixing bowl. Set it aside until required.

To prepare the langoustine, pull off the heads from them while they are still alive, and then remove the centre vein. Do this by clasping the centre fin of the tail between your thumb and forefinger, twist and then pull, bringing the whole intestinal tract with it. This only works if the langoustine is very fresh. Alternatively, get your fishmonger to do it. Lay the tails belly-down on a chopping block and, using a sharp knife, cut them in half along their length taking out any veins that are left behind. Place the halves, shell-side down on a tray and sprinkle over half of the marinade. Leave for a minimum of 30 minutes and maximum of 3 hours.

Cook the noodles for four minutes, just until they are tender but with a wee bit off a bite in them.

Then drain the noodles well. Stir the sesame oil straight away into the noodles. Get them nice and mixed, use your fingers. The aim is to get all of the strands lightly coated with the oil so that they don't all stick together. Then stir in the other half of the leftover marinade, the finely chopped spring onions and the fresh coriander. Keep noodles warm.

Heat a ribbed grill pan (or a barbecue) until it's nice and hot. Then take the langoustine, liberally coated in the marinade, and pop them on the grill, flesh side down for about two minutes then turn them over and leave for another minute shell-side down.

Serve the noodles in nice deep bowls with the langoustine scattered all over the top.

Cooking time: 15 minutes

Potpie

Phillip Schofield - Actor, TV Personality

Ingredients - Serves 6

2 medium potatoes, diced
1 large onion, diced
1 leek, sliced
1 small green pepper, diced
1 small red pepper, diced
1 small yellow pepper, diced
1 small packet baby corn or small tin corn
1 packet ready made puff pastry
1 tin or carton Vichyssoise mushroom or chicken soup

2 medium carrots, diced
4 spring onions, diced
1 parsnip, diced
1 courgette, diced
½ lb diced turkey or chicken
½ lb mushrooms, sliced
2 stock cubes
seasoning

Method

Preheat oven to 190°C/375°F/gas mark 5

Lightly fry the onion together with the turkey for about 7-8 minutes. Place all the other vegetables except the mushrooms in a large ovenproof dish. Then add the cooked onion and turkey mix. Sprinkle with 2 stock cubes of your favourite flavour and add ¾ of a pint of water. Cover and place in a medium oven for 1 hour. Then add sliced mushrooms, soup, a sprinkling of basil and coriander. Cover the pie with the rolled out pastry, seal the edges to stop the pie juices coming out of the edges. Place back in the oven for 20 minutes or until the pastry is well-risen and golden brown. With this pie you can add or leave out any vegetables you choose, but a varied selection is advised and the potatoes do act as a thickener.

Cooking time: 2 hours 30 minutes

The Great Michael
Photograph courtesy of Joyce Higginson

The warship The Great Michael was constructed, utilising wood from the forests of Fife, in the 1511. A model was built by the crew to show their appreciation for the help that was given to them by the local people when the ship foundered off the coast of Burntisland. The model that hangs in the church today is a copy of the original model which was lost whilst the church was being renovated in 1822.

Patrick's Saucy Sauce for Pasta

Patrick Anthony - Celebrity Chef, "Ready Steady Cook"

"With best wishes and compliments."

Ingredients - Serves 2-4

3 tablespoons olive oil
4 rashers lean smoked bacon, cut into pieces
2 tablespoons parsley, finely chopped
2 tablespoons freshly grated Parmesan cheese
salt and pepper to taste (watch salt because of bacon)
1 level teaspoon dried chilli flakes (use less for milder sauce)

1 measure vodka
4 tablespoons cream
15 oz can chopped tomatoes
2 cloves garlic, crushed
roasted pepper strips (optional)

Method

Heat oil in pan. Add bacon and allow to colour. Then add garlic and stir through. Add tomatoes, chilli flakes and vodka. Mix everything thoroughly and simmer for 15 minutes. Stir in the cream, seasoning and parsley and stir through. Then add the cheese and the optional roasted pepper strips if used. Stir again and serve. **Cooking time: 30 minutes**

Braised Shin of Beef with Chinese Spices

Paul Rankin - Celebrity Chef, "Ready Steady Cook"

Ingredients - Serves 4

2 lb shin of beef, cut into 1 inch thick cubes
2 pints water
6 star anise
6 fl oz medium sherry
6 garlic cloves, finely sliced
1½ inch piece of ginger, peeled and finely sliced
3½ fl oz dark soy sauce
6 tablespoons soft brown sugar
1 teaspoon salt

Garnish:

1 small bunch coriander, roughly chopped
1 small bunch spring onion, finely chopped

Method

Place the shin of beef in the water, and bring to the boil over medium high heat. Lower the heat and simmer for ½ hour. Skim frequently to remove any scum. Add the remaining ingredients and simmer partially covered for another 3 hours. By now, the meat should be very tender. Uncover the pot and cook until the sauce is reduced, and slightly syrupy.

Serve with steamed Jasmine rice, or Basmati rice, and garlic Bok Choy. Sprinkle with the coriander and spring onion, just before serving.

Cooking time: 4 hours

Chicken Cacciatore

John W. McDougall JP - Convener, Fife Council

Ingredients - Serves 4-6

2 lb chicken parts
2 tablespoons flour
2 tablespoons oil
10 oz can condensed tomato soup
¾ tea cup dry red wine
1 teacup mushrooms, sliced

1 medium onion, sliced
½ teaspoon each basil, oregano, salt
2 cloves garlic, minced
1 bay leaf
1 green pepper, sliced

Method

Coat chicken with flour. In a large frying pan, brown chicken in oil. Add remaining ingredients, except pepper and mushrooms. Stir well, cover, and simmer for 30 minutes. Add green pepper and mushrooms. Cook for a further 15 minutes. Remove bay leaf.

Serve with noodles or spaghetti.

Cooking time: 1 hour

Spanish Style Chicken Breast in Wine Vinegar

Margaret Wilson - West Calder

Ingredients - Serves 4

2 chicken breasts boned and without skin
4 glasses of olive oil or other vegetable oil
1 head of garlic, the cloves peeled but whole
1 onion cut in quarters
2 large carrots, sliced

1 bay leaf
thyme
freshly ground pepper
2 glasses of wine vinegar

Method

Boil the carrots for about 10 minutes. Salt the chicken breasts. Put all the ingredients in a pot and simmer gently (on a hot plate, not in the oven) for about 1½ hours. Slice the chicken diagonally. Note: the "glass measure" is rather vague but the important thing is the proportion i.e. 1 part vinegar to 2 parts oil, and that the oil and vinegar mix completely covers the chicken.

Cooking time: 1 hour 40 minutes

Thai Tuna with Lemon Grass and Ginger

Helen Robertson - Carnock

Ingredients - Serves 4

1 kaffir lime leaf
3 tablespoons coarse sea salt
5 tablespoons soft brown sugar
4 tuna steaks, approx 8oz each
1 stalk lemon grass, sliced into thin rounds

1 inch piece root ginger, cut into matchsticks
1 lime
1 tablespoon vegetable oil
1 large ripe avocado, peeled and stoned
salt and freshly ground black pepper

Method

To make the marinade, bruise the lime leaf by crushing slightly, to release the flavour. Process the sea salt, brown sugar and lime leaf together in a food processor until thoroughly blended. Place the tuna steaks in a bowl. Sprinkle the marinade over them and add the lemon grass and ginger. Leave for 3-4 hours to marinate. Rinse off the marinade and pat dry with kitchen paper. Peel the lime.
Remove any excess pith from the peel, then cut into very thin strips. Heat the wok, then add the oil. When the oil is hot, add the lime rind and then the steaks and fry for 3-4 minutes. Add the juice of the lime. Remove from the heat, slice the avocado and add to the fish. Season and serve.
Note: Swordfish is good instead of Tuna if you can get it.

Cooking time: 15 minutes

Maria Contini's Spaghettini with Tomato Sugo

Valvona and Crolla Delicatessen - Edinburgh

Ingredients - Serves 4

12 oz-1lb Spaghettini (thin spaghetti)
3 tablespoons olive oil
2 cloves garlic, peeled and sliced or chopped
1½-2 lb plum tomatoes, skinned, de-seeded and coarsely chopped
small handful of fresh basil leaves
salt and freshly ground black pepper
freshly grated Parmesan cheese to serve

Method

Bring a large pan of salted water to the boil. Add the spaghettini. As soon as the pasta is in the pan, heat the olive oil in a large frying pan over a brisk heat, and add the garlic. Stir for about 30 seconds, then add the tomatoes. Stir and simmer, then leave to bubble, occasionally crushing down the tomatoes, for 5 minutes or so, until they form a rough sauce. Season with salt and pepper, then roughly tear the basil leaves and scatter over the sauce. Cook for 1 minute or so more. Taste and adjust seasoning. Drain the pasta and tip into the sauce, if there's enough room in the pan. If not, tip the sauce over the pasta in the usual way. Turn carefully, to coat, then serve with freshly grated Parmesan.

Cooking time: 10-15 minutes

Roast Rib of Beef with a Horseradish and Coriander Crust, Roast Potatoes, Yorkshire Pudding and Roasted Vegetables

Brian J. Turner - Celebrity Chef, "Ready Steady Cook"

"All the very best for such a worthwhile project"

Ingredients - Serves 8

5 lb rib of beef
mustard
horseradish cream
breadcrumbs
coriander
salt and pepper

Yorkshire Puddings:

1 cup plain flour
1 cup milk
3 eggs
pinch of salt
1 teaspoon vinegar
oil

Method

Preheat oven to 240°C/475°F/gas mark 9
Trim the excess nerve and fat from inside the beef. Roast the beef on a bed of vegetables, potatoes, parsnips, carrots and onions for the first 20 minutes, this helps to give the joint a good crust and gets the cooking off to a good start. Mix the horseradish and mustard together, remove the beef and brush the back of the beef liberally with the mixture. Push on the breadcrumbs mixed with salt and pepper and coriander. Lower the oven to 190°C/375°F/gas mark 5 and roast using the following times/weight depending on your taste: 14 minutes per lb for Rare / 21 minutes per lb for Medium / 27 minutes per lb for Well Done. Take the beef out of the oven and rest for 20 minutes before slicing.

Yorkshire puddings:
Break eggs into bowl and lightly mix. Add half the water and milk, add the flour and 1 teaspoon salt. Mix to smooth paste. Add the rest of the liquor and allow to rest for 2-3 hours if possible.
Put Yorkshire pudding tins into the oven with dripping to get very hot. Pour in the mixture and cook at about 240°C/475°F/gas mark 9 for approximately 20 minutes until cooked. Serve immediately.
Cooking time: 1 hour 50 minutes

Braised Pheasant with Whisky and Juniper

Josephine Quinney - Burntisland

Ingredients - Serves 2

1 2½ lb pheasant
2 tablespoons oil or butter
1 medium onion, finely chopped
1 tablespoon juniper berries
¼ pint game stock or water

4 fl oz whisky
4 fl oz whipping cream
1 teaspoon lemon juice
salt and pepper

Method

Preheat oven to 190°C/375°F/gas mark 5
Melt the fat or oil in an oven-proof casserole and brown the pheasant on all sides. Remove and add the onions and cook until golden brown. Return the pheasant to the pan and pour over half the whisky. Flambé and when the flames die down, add the stock and juniper berries. Cover well and bake in the oven for 45 minutes or until tender. Remove the bird and cut into four equal pieces. Keep the joints warm on a serving dish. Strain the juices and return to the pan. Add the remaining whisky, cream and lemon juice and reduce until the sauce is thickened. Season and pour over the joints of the pheasant. Serve with new potatoes and green vegetables.
Cooking time: 1 hour 15 minutes

"Willie Muir"
Postcard courtesy of Alan Barker

The Burntisland to Granton Ferry commenced in 1844. With the completion of the railway link northwards, the first rail ferry in the world was built and made the crossing to Burntisland on 1st March 1850.The "William Muir" maintained a regular service from Granton to Burntisland until 1937.

Spiced Roast Leg of Lamb

Ingredients - Serves 8

4 lb leg of lamb, trimmed
5 oz fresh ginger
8-10 cloves garlic, peeled
2 green chillies, chopped
2 teaspoons cumin seeds
20 whole cloves
1 teaspoon peppercorns
3 large cardamoms

8 small green cardamoms
3 tablespoons lemon juice
1 tablespoon vinegar
¼ pint natural yoghurt
½ teaspoon chilli powder
2 teaspoons ground coriander
2 teaspoons paprika
3-4 sprigs coriander leaves
salt

To garnish:
lime slices, fresh mint sprigs and fried onion rings

Method

Preheat oven to 200°C/400°F/gas mark 6

Put the ginger, garlic, green chillies, cumin seeds, cloves, peppercorns, large and small cardamoms and coriander leaves with the lemon juice in a blender or food processor and work to a smooth paste. Mix in the vinegar and yoghurt, then add the chilli powder, coriander and paprika. Make 1 inch deep cuts across the meat and sprinkle with salt. Put the lamb in a bowl, pour over the spice and yoghurt mixture and rub it into the cuts. Cover with cling film and leave to marinate in the refrigerator for 48 hours.

Take the lamb out of the refrigerator and place in a large flameproof casserole with the marinade. Bring to the boil on top of the cooker.

Transfer to the preheated oven and bake uncovered for 30 minutes. Reduce the oven temperature to 170°C/325°F/gas mark 3. Cover and cook for 3½ hours, basting occasionally. Remove the meat from the casserole and keep on a serving dish covered with foil. Put the casserole on top of the cooker, skim off any fat from the top, and simmer the sauce until thick. Pour over the lamb. Carve, garnish and serve.

Cooking time: 4 hours

Roast Duckling

Terry Wogan - TV Personality, "Children In Need"

"A favourite recipe of my wife, Helen and I is roast duckling. We always use the Delia Smith method, which we find quite foolproof."

Ingredients see method - Serves 2

Method

Preheat the oven to 220°C/425°F/gas mark 7

You need a half duckling per person. For two people you would need a duck weighing about 4 1bs, as well as some salt and freshly ground black pepper to season. The secret is not to put any fat on the duck, just prick it all over with a skewer, going deep into the flesh, and put a rack in the roasting tin and place the tin on a high shelf in the oven. After 20 minutes, turn the heat down to 180°C/350°F/gas mark 4, then all you have do is leave it alone for two hours. For the gravy, simmer some chicken stock with the giblets from the duck for quite a while to give it a good flavour. When the duck is ready, remove all the fat except for a dessert teaspoon and the nice brown bits in the roasting tin. Then add one dessert teaspoon of flour and cook the roux for a few minutes to brown it, add the strained stock and stir until smooth. Then add red wine and two dessert tablespoons of red currant jelly, which gives it a nice flavour. The result is a lovely, aromatic dish. **Cooking time: 2 hours 20 minutes**

Char Grilled Grey Mullet with a Warm Chilli and Coriander Dressing

Aberdour Hotel - Aberdour

Ingredients - Serves 4

Fish:	Dressing:
4 fresh fillets of grey mullet	100 ml extra virgin olive oil
salt and pepper	1 small red chilli
olive oil	1 heaped tablespoon freshly chopped coriander
	zest and juice of one lime
	black pepper

Method

Dressing: De-seed the red chilli, dice finely and add to olive oil. Mix in fresh coriander, zest and juice of lime and black pepper. Cover and set aside.

Preheat barbecue, griddle pan or grill to medium hot.

Brush fillets of grey mullet with olive oil and season with salt and pepper. Place skin side down on barbecue or griddle (skin side up on grill) Cook for 2-3 minutes then turn and cook for another 2-3 minutes. Turn fillet through 90 degrees, still flesh side down, and cook for 2-3 minutes more. Push gently down on thickest part of fillet. If it gives slightly, it is ready to serve.

Heat dressing gently in a pan, do not boil. Place fish on a warm plate and drizzle some warm dressing over the top. Serve with a fresh green salad and crusty bread.

Cooking time: 15 minutes

Haggis stuffed Turkey

Jimmy Logan - Scottish Comedian

Ingredients - Serves 6

6-8 lb turkey	1 onion, diced
haggis	sliced apples
butter or oil	½ lb sausage meat stuffing
sliced bananas	½ pkt sage and onion stuffing mix

Method

Preheat oven to 170°C/325°F/gas mark 3

Take the haggis out of its skin or tin. Break the haggis up into a large bowl. Fry onion with a little butter or oil in a pan and when they are soft add sultanas, sliced bananas and sliced apples. The fruit will give plenty of juice, so you can discard this. Gently fry the haggis and some sausage meat and when it is cooked you can add the stuffing mix. Then add to the fruit and onion and mix well. Stuff the turkey and cook at for 3-3½ hours or until the juices run clear when pricked with a skewer. As you may have too much stuffing you may need to cook what you cannot get into the bird in a separate oven dish.

Cooking time: 3-3½ hours

Garlic and Rosemary Lamb with a Red Wine Gravy

Fern Britton - TV Personality, "Ready Steady Cook"

"I don't know what I would do without roast lamb. I even have it for Christmas. This is a very rich variation of a basic Sunday lunch but boy is it good! The flavours of rosemary, garlic and red wine are perfect companions to the lamb. The addition of anchovies may sound a bit odd but they act as a tenderiser and any fishy flavour is cooked out".

Ingredients - Serves 6-8

5½ lb leg of lamb
3 cloves of garlic
3 large sprigs of rosemary
4 tinned anchovy fillets
9 fl oz (half a bottle) red wine
1 tablespoon plain flour
a little stock or vegetable water
salt and pepper

Method

Preheat oven to 190°C/375°F/gas mark 5

Trim off as much fat as you can from the leg of lamb. Using a small sharp knife make several cuts about 1 inch deep into both sides of the meat. Slice the garlic cloves lengthways into thin slivers. Divide the rosemary into small sprigs and cut the anchovies into ½ inch strips. Insert a piece each of garlic, rosemary and anchovy into the cuts, squashing in the anchovy. Place lamb in a non metallic dish, pour a glass of red wine over the meat and leave to marinate for at least 30 minutes, but better still overnight, covered up in the fridge. Place the lamb on a rack in a roasting tray. Pour the marinade juices over the lamb and season with salt and pepper. Roast the lamb for 20 minutes per pound to give you lamb that is just cooked but not well done. Add a splash more red wine during cooking but save about 3/4 of a glass for the gravy. Take the lamb out of the oven, put it on a warmed platter, cover with foil and leave to stand for 15-20 minutes before carving. Meanwhile make the gravy using the juices in the roasting tray. Spoon off most of the excess fat. Put the roasting pan over a gentle heat. Sprinkle on the flour and whisk into the remaining fat. I find using a small whisk produces the best results for lump-free gravy. Pour in the remaining wine and scrape any sediment from the bottom of the pan and stir in. Add vegetable water or stock to the pan, a little at a time and simmer. Keep whisking until the gravy has thickened. Check the seasoning, pour the gravy into a warmed jug and serve.

Cooking time: 1 hour 40 minutes

Enjoy!

Smoked Haddock and Mushroom Gougere

Janet Barr - Glenrothes

Ingredients - Serves 4

8 oz smoked haddock fillet
½ pint milk
1 onion, finely chopped
1 carrot, finely chopped
8 oz button mushrooms, finely chopped

1 oz cornflour
2 teaspoons fresh parsley, chopped
2 teaspoons fresh chives, chopped
salt and black pepper

Method

Place the haddock, milk, onion and carrot in a saucepan. Bring to a gentle simmer, then cover and cook for 7-8 minutes or until the fish flakes easily. Lift out the fish onto a board and flake into pieces, discarding the skin and any bones. Add the mushrooms to the milk and cover. Cook for a further 2 minutes. Blend the cornflour with a little water then mix into the sauce. Stir continuously until the mixture thickens. Add the parsley and chives then fold in the haddock flakes, season with salt and pepper to taste.
Spoon into an ovenproof dish and bake for 35-40 minutes until golden brown.
Cooking time: 60 minutes

Danish Steaks with Pernod

Gillian Braid - Burntisland

Ingredients - Serves 6

2 oz butter
1 large onion, thinly sliced
1¼ lb gammon steak, cubed
2 teaspoons cornflour
juice of ½ lemon

½ teaspoon dried tarragon
1 Granny Smith apple, cored and sliced
5 fl oz double cream
1 small glass of white wine
pepper

Method

Fry onion in butter until it is soft. Toss gammon in cornflour and add to onion and cook for 5-6 minutes. Combine lemon juice, Pernod, tarragon and pepper with the white wine, pour over the gammon stir well and cook for 15 minutes. Add apple and cook for another 5 minutes, or until the meat is tender. Stir in the cream and serve on a bed of pasta or rice.
Cooking time: 35 minutes

Tuna Pasta Salad

Lesley Braid - Burntisland

Ingredients - Serves 4

250 g pasta (shells or bows are best)
185 g tuna in brine, drained
fresh tomatoes, diced
cucumber, diced
4 spring onions, chopped

green and yellow pepper, de-seeded and diced
2-3 tablespoons mayonnaise
salt and pepper to taste
½ teaspoon paprika

Method

Cook pasta as per instructions on pack and allow to cool. Place the drained tuna in a large bowl, add pasta, tomatoes, cucumber, peppers and spring onions. Add salt and pepper, then mix in the mayonnaise (add a little more if required). Sprinkle the paprika over the tuna salad, cover with cling film and chill in fridge until ready for use. Serve on its own or with a fresh green salad and crusty bread.

Cooking time: 15 minutes

Divers being picked up after a dive
Trust divers work at a high tide dive depth of around 30 metres. Visibility at this depth is anything from 30cm to 2 metres

Chicken Curry

Lawson Brand - Burntisland Community Award Winner 1995

Ingredients - Serves 4

4 chicken breasts
oil or butter
2 large onions, finely sliced
2 tomatoes
8 green chillies, finely sliced

4 cloves garlic, crushed
1 teaspoon salt
1 teaspoon paprika powder
½ teaspoon daniya
1 teaspoon garam masala

Method

On a high heat add enough oil to line the bottom of your cooking pot. Add onions, tomatoes and green chillies and fry gently for about 5 minutes. Then add the garlic and enough water to cook the mixture until the onions become soft. Now add the salt, paprika, daniya and ½ teaspoon of the garam masala. Stir then add the chicken to the pot, and add about half a mug of water and cover pot. Turn up the heat until the curry starts to simmer and stir occasionally to stop the curry from sticking. Cook for 30 minutes adding more water if required. Add the remaining garam masala and cook on for a further 30 minutes. You will know when the curry is ready when the onions disappear and form the base of the sauce. Once cooked sprinkle with chopped herbs and serve with boiled rice.

Cooking time: 1 hour 20 minutes

Chicken Divan

Catherine Millar - Dunfermline

Ingredients - Serves 4-6

1 lb broccoli
1 oz flour
1 oz butter
4 small chicken breasts, cooked and sliced
¼ pint chicken stock
¼ pint double cream

3 tablespoons sherry
salt and pepper
4 oz cheddar cheese, grated
2 tablespoons Parmesan cheese
1 small tin peaches

Method

Preheat oven to 180°C/350°F/gas mark 4
Cook broccoli in salted boiling water, drain and arrange on the base of a casserole dish.
Melt butter in a pan, and blend in the flour. Add the chicken stock and cook until the mixture thickens. Stir in the cream, sherry, salt and pepper into the sauce. Pour half the sauce over the broccoli and top with the sliced chicken. Add half the cheddar and 1 tablespoon of Parmesan cheese to the sauce, then pour over the chicken. Sprinkle the remaining cheese over the top of the dish and bake in a hot oven for 20 minutes. Garnish with sliced peaches. **Cooking time: 40 minutes**

Gammon Steaks in a Cheese Sauce

Catherine Millar - Dunfermline

Ingredients - Serves 4

4 gammon steaks
1 lb fresh spinach
1 oz butter
4 fl oz chicken stock

4 fl oz sour cream
2 oz grated smoked cheese
pinch ground nutmeg
salt and pepper

Method

Preheat oven to 190°C/375°F/gas mark 5
Cook gammon steaks in tin foil with the butter for 30 minutes. Cook spinach in a small amount of water for 5 minutes, drain and leave aside. Add stock to pan and reduce a little, turn heat down and add the cream, spinach, nutmeg, cheese and seasoning. Heat through for 1 minute. Pour mixture over the gammon steaks and serve with fresh vegetables.
Cooking time: 40 minutes

Cheddar Style Pork

Kathleen Robertson - Burntisland

Ingredients - Serves 4

4 pork fillets or chops
1 oz butter
6 oz mushrooms

6 oz Cheddar cheese
¼ pint apple juice, unsweetened
4 tablespoons breadcrumbs

Method

Preheat oven to 200°C/400°F/gas mark 6
Butter a large, shallow, ovenproof dish. Chop mushrooms and arrange on the bottom of the dish. Place pork on top of mushrooms and pour over the apple juice. Mix the cheese with the breadcrumbs and scatter on top of the meat making sure that it is covered. Bake in the oven for 45 minutes or until pork is tender.
Cooking time: 45 minutes

Smoked Fish Pie

Anthea Turner - TV Personality

Ingredients - Serves 4

1½ lb smoked haddock
4 kipper fillets, weighing a total 4-6 oz
1 pint milk
4 oz butter
1 bay leaf
2 oz flour
2 hard-boiled eggs, roughly chopped
3 tablespoons fresh chopped parsley
1 tablespoon capers (can be left out if not available)
1 tablespoon lemon juice
salt and freshly milled black pepper

Topping:
2 lb fresh boiled potatoes
2 oz butter
4 tablespoons milk
freshly grated nutmeg
1 oz strong cheddar cheese, grated

Method

Preheat the oven to 200°C/400°F/gas mark 6

Arrange fish in a baking tin, pour half the milk over it, add a few flecks of the butter and the bay leaf, and then bake in the oven for 15-20 minutes. Pour off and reserve the cooking liquid, then remove the skin from the fish and flake the flesh into largish pieces.

Next make the sauce by melting the remaining butter in a saucepan, then stirring in the flour and gradually adding the fish liquid bit by bit, stirring well after each addition. When all the liquid is in, finish the sauce by gradually adding the remaining milk, seasoning with salt and pepper and simmering for 3-4 minutes. Now mix the fish into the sauce, together with the hard boiled eggs, parsley and capers, then taste to see if it needs any more seasoning and stir in the lemon juice.

Pour the mixture into a buttered baking dish (about 2½ pints).

Next prepare the topping. Cream the potatoes, starting off with a large fork, then finishing off with an electric beater, if you have one, adding the butter and milk. Season the potatoes with salt and pepper and add some freshly grated nutmeg, spread evenly over the fish then sprinkle with cheese. Bake on a high shelf in the oven, still at 200°C/400°F/gas mark 6 for about 30 minutes, by which time the pie will be heated through and the top will be nicely brown. **Cooking time: 1 hour**

Meat Loaf

Archie Robertson - Burntisland Community Award Winner 1987.

Archie was a "weel kent face" in Burntisland.
This recipe is dedicated to his memory.

Ingredients - Serves 4-6

1 lb minced beef
4 fl oz milk
2 oz breadcrumbs
1 medium onion, chopped

2 oz porridge oats
2 oz tomato ketchup
pinch of nutmeg
salt and pepper

Method

Preheat oven to 180°C/350°F/gas mark 4

Put the porridge oats, milk, egg, onion, nutmeg and seasoning in a bowl. Mix well and allow to stand for 5 minutes. Mix in the mince thoroughly. Place the mixture in an 8½ x 4½ x 2½ inch greased loaf tin. Cover top of the mixture with tomato ketchup and coat well with breadcrumbs. Bake in the oven for approximately 1 hour, until the crust has turned brown and the loaf is bubbling.
Cooking time: 1 hour

Oven Baked Lemon Chicken

Aberdour Hotel - Aberdour

Ingredients - Serves 4

4 large chicken breasts
8 very ripe lemons
1 small red chilli

1 clove of garlic
2 tablespoons of honey
salt and pepper

Method

Preheat oven to 190°C/375°F/gas mark 5

De-seed the red chilli and dice finely. Halve the lemons and squeeze the juice. Crush and chop the garlic. Mix the chilli and garlic with the honey. Place the chicken in an ovenproof dish, pour the marinade over the top. Tuck half of the squeezed lemon skins around the chicken. Leave in fridge for at least 2 hours. Cover dish and place in oven for 20 minutes or until chicken is cooked. Remove lid and cook for 5 more minutes to add colour. Serve with boiled rice and hot Ciabatta bread.

Cooking time: 30 minutes

Potted Hough - II

Wm. Cameron - Local Butcher, Burntisland

Bob Fairley - Heritage Trust Volunteer

Ingredients - Serves 6

3 lb hough (shin beef)
nap bone (knucklebone)

water
salt and pepper

Method

Wash the bone and the meat. Place hough and nap bone in pan. Cover with water and bring to the boil. Simmer for 2½ hours. Chop or mince the meat and some of the gel of the bone together. Place back in pan, season with salt and pepper to taste and simmer for a further 30-45 minutes. Allow to cool and place in dish to set. Serve with mashed potatoes and mashed swede.

Cooking time: 3 hours 30 minutes

Baked Macaroni (Maltese style)

Ingredients - Serves 6

400g macaroni
2 hard boiled eggs, roughly chopped
600ml stock
100g onions, chopped
seasoning

50g tomato paste
50g grated cheese
200g minced meat
3 eggs, beaten
oil

Method

Preheat oven to 180°C/350°F/gas mark 4

Fry the onions in a little oil until they are golden, then add the meat and continue cooking until it is brown. Add the tomato paste and stock and cook for a further 20 minutes until liquid has reduced a little. Boil the macaroni in plenty of salted water. When this is ready, drain off the water. Add the meat sauce, cheese, hard-boiled eggs and the seasoning to the macaroni. Blend in the beaten eggs and place into an oiled pie dish. Bake in the oven for 30-40 minutes. Serve with a fresh green salad and crusty bread.

Cooking time: 1 hour

Courgettes in a Creamy Garlic Sauce

Ingredients - Serves 4

8 oz courgettes
4 oz mushrooms
5 fl oz natural yoghurt
2 oz cream cheese with garlic and herbs

½ oz butter
1 tablespoon oil
salt and pepper

Method

Melt butter and oil, gently fry courgettes and mushrooms for 5-7 minutes stirring frequently, season to taste and place in serving dish and keep warm. Mix together cheese and yoghurt, heat gently in a small pan, then pour over the vegetables.

Cooking time: 15 minutes

Broccoli and Macaroni Casserole

Aileen Braid - Heritage Trust Volunteer

Ingredients - Serves 4

8 oz macaroni
salt and pepper
1 lb broccoli
14 oz can chopped tomatoes
1 large onion, chopped

1 clove garlic, crushed
1 teaspoon dried oregano
10 fl oz plain yoghurt
4 oz soft cream cheese
2 tablespoons cornflakes

Method

Preheat oven to 200°C/400°F/gas mark 6

Cook macaroni, drain and keep warm. Trim broccoli, cook until just tender and drain. Place tomatoes, onion, garlic and oregano in a pan, season with salt and pepper. Simmer until onions are tender. Put a layer of tomato sauce into an ovenproof dish, cover with a layer of cooked macaroni then a layer of broccoli. Repeat layers until all ingredients are used up. Beat together yoghurt and cheese, season and spread over casserole. Bake for 30 minutes or until bubbling and golden brown. Sprinkle with cornflakes and serve.

Cooking time: 50 minutes

Carrot and Parsnip Purée with Cheese

Ingredients - Serves 4-6

1½ lb carrots
1 lb parsnips
3 oz butter

grated nutmeg
salt and pepper
4 oz grated cheese

Method

Cook carrots and parsnips till soft. Process or mash, add butter, nutmeg and seasoning. Process or mash again until mixture resembles a purée. Spoon into a gratin dish, sprinkle with grated cheese and season with pepper. Grill until cheese has melted and is golden brown.

Cooking time: 30 minutes

Cauliflower Bake

Ingredients - Serves 4-6

6 eggs
1 lb leeks thinly sliced
½ lb green beans
6 oz grated cheese

1 medium cauliflower in sprigs
½ pint single cream
1 teaspoon mustard
salt and pepper

Method

Preheat the oven to 180°C/350°F/gas mark 4
Prepare vegetables and cook in salted water for 10 minutes then strain. Butter casserole dish, add hot vegetables and most of the cheese. Whisk eggs with seasoning and cream. Pour over vegetables. Sprinkle with remaining cheese. Cover and bake for 30 minutes.
Cooking time: 45 minutes

Sandcastle competition on the Beach
Postcard courtesy of Alan Barker

Baked Pepper and Chutney Pots

Ingredients - Serves 6

1 dessertspoon olive oil
1 oz butter
8 oz finely chopped onions
2 oz finely chopped red pepper
1 tablespoon chutney, any variety

½ teaspoon caster sugar
salt and pepper
6 teaspoons grated Parmesan cheese
7 oz Greek yoghurt
2 size 3 eggs plus 1 yolk, beaten

Method

Preheat oven to 180°C/350°F/gas mark 4.
Fry onion and pepper in the oil and butter till soft, then remove from heat. When cool mix with remaining ingredients and divide into six 4 inch ramekin dishes. Place in a roasting tin filled with a little warm water and cook for 30 minutes until set. Serve immediately.
Cooking time: 30 minutes

Spinach Salad

Wendy Hurley - New Jersey, USA

Ingredients - Serves as prepared

as many baby spinach leaves as you require.
poppy seed dressing. (bought in supermarkets)

strawberries cut into slices
1 packet sliced almonds

Method

You will need a large wooden salad bowl. Place the spinach leaves in the bowl, add cut strawberries and as much poppy seed dressing as required for personal taste, it should just coat the leaves and not make them soggy. Sprinkle the almonds on the top.

Cooking time: nil

Roast Potatoes and Shallots with Sun Dried Tomatoes

Aileen Braid - Heritage Trust Volunteer

Ingredients - Serves 6

8 oz shallots
1 lb small new potatoes
4 cloves garlic
5 pieces sun dried tomatoes

3 tablespoons olive oil
2 teaspoons balsamic vinegar
2 teaspoons chopped thyme
salt and pepper

Method

Preheat oven to 190°C/375°F/gas mark 5.
Pour boiling water over shallots, leave for 2 minutes then drain and peel. When cool make crosscuts through the shallots almost to the root. Scrub and dry potatoes. Place shallots, potatoes and garlic in a medium sized roasting tin. Mix well, drizzle over 2 tablespoon of oil from tomatoes along with the olive oil. Drizzle over vinegar, sprinkle with thyme and season. Bake for 45 minutes turning half way through cooking until crisp and golden.

Cooking time: 45 minutes

Baked Beans Greek Style

Costa & Jo Sofianos - A-Z Cleaning Services, Burntisland

Ingredients - Serves 6-8

1 lb haricot or butter beans
2 tins chopped tomatoes
6 medium carrots diced
1 large onion, finely chopped
4 fl oz olive oil

2 sticks of celery, finely sliced
1 red pepper, finely chopped
1 green pepper, finely chopped
2 tablespoons flat parsley, chopped
salt and black pepper

Method

Soak beans overnight in cold water, then drain and rinse. Boil beans in salted water for 30 minutes and drain again. Return beans to pan, add carrots, tomatoes, olive oil, celery, red and green peppers and the parsley, season to taste. Simmer for 1 hour 30 minutes stirring occasionally to stop beans from sticking and until tender. Serve with any type of fish, black olives and a Greek salad.

Cooking time: approximately 2 hours

Tomato Summer Pudding

Joyce Higginson - Burntisland Community Award Winner 2000

Ingredients - Serves 6-8

6 slices of bread, crusts removed
2 tins chopped tomatoes
bunch of chopped basil
¼ green pepper

¼ yellow pepper
¼ chopped red onion
salt and pepper
½ of a lime jelly, dissolved in 2½ fl oz water

Method

Drain the tomatoes and reserve the juice. Soak the bread in the tomato juice and line a pudding bowl with the slices of bread. Place the strained tomatoes, basil, peppers, lime jelly and red onion in a separate bowl and mix together. Season to taste. Fill the bread-lined basin with the tomato mixture and place another slice of bread dipped in the tomato juice on the top. Weight down with a saucer or plate with a heavy object on top. Place in fridge until set. Decorate with a tomato rose and parsley sprigs. Serve with a summer buffet.

Cooking time: nil

Caesar Salad

Wendy Hurley - New Jersey, USA

Ingredients - Serves 8

3 garlic cloves
3 anchovy fillets
1 rounded teaspoon salt
½ teaspoon dry mustard
dash of Worcestershire sauce
2 tablespoons wine vinegar
¾ cup olive oil

1 raw egg
juice of one lemon
2 heads romaine (cos) lettuce
12 cherry tomatoes
1 cup croutons
½ cup fresh grated Parmesan cheese

Method

You will need a large wooden salad bowl, food processor or blender. Process the garlic and anchovies together until they are in a puréed state. Add salt, dry mustard, Worcestershire sauce, vinegar, olive oil, egg and lemon juice. Process until the dressing is well blended. Wash and dry the romaine leaves, then break them into a large wooden salad bowl. Add tomatoes and croutons. Toss the salad in the dressing. Sprinkle the Parmesan cheese on top of the salad. Toss and serve salad immediately. This is often served as a 'starter' in the USA but can be eaten along with the entrée as you wish.

Cooking time: nil

Turnip Surprise

Tony Robinson - Actor "Blackadder"

"Best Wishes"

Mr. S. Baldrick (BLACKADDER) has asked me to send the following recipe to you for possible inclusion in your recipe book.

1. Hide behind a door.
2. Wait till a turnip comes in.
3. Say "Boo".

Asian Coleslaw

Paul Rankin - Celebrity Chef, "Ready Steady Cook"

Ingredients - Serves 4-6

9 oz white cabbage, shredded
1 small carrot, finely grated
2 tablespoons pickled ginger, finely chopped
4 tablespoons fresh coriander, roughly chopped
2 tablespoons spring onion, finely sliced

1 tablespoon sugar
2 tablespoons lime juice
½ teaspoon chilli powder
3-4 tablespoons soy sauce
1 tablespoon peanut butter

Method

Combine the cabbage, carrot, and ginger together in a ceramic bowl. Mix in a separate bowl the soy, peanut butter, sugar, lime juice, and the chilli powder. Add this to the cabbage mixture, and leave to marinate for at least 1 hour, and no longer than 3. Just before serving, toss in the coriander and spring onions.

Cooking time: nil

Bok Choy, with Garlic

Jeanne Rankin - Celebrity Chef, "Ready Steady Cook"

Ingredients - Serves 4-6

1 lb Bok Choy, or other Chinese greens
2 tablespoons vegetable oil

2 teaspoons chopped garlic
½ teaspoon salt

Method

Trim the Bok Choy and cut into large bite size pieces. Heat the oil in a wok or large frying pan until almost smoking. Add the garlic, and the salt. Stir-fry for about 10 seconds, and then add the Bok Choy. Cook for about 1 minute or until the greens are just *al dente*. Serve at once.

Cooking time: 3 minutes

Courgette Flan

Michael Aspel -TV Personality, "This is Your Life"

"I hope the Burntisland project is a great success."

Ingredients - Serves 6

flan case
6 oz cheddar cheese
salt and pepper
1 lb courgettes

3 eggs
¼ pint milk
1 onion

Method

Preheat the oven to 190°C/375°F/gas mark 5

Slice courgettes and fry in oil with onion for 10 minutes. Whisk together 3 eggs and the milk. Grate cheese. Place courgettes and onion in flan case and cover with milk and eggs. Finally sprinkle with cheese. Place in pre-heated oven for 50-60 minutes.

(For variation: add a few prawns or chopped crispy bacon.)

Cooking time: 50-60 minutes

Quick Fried Rice

Carol Vorderman - TV Presenter, "Countdown".

"Wishing you every success."

Ingredients - Serves 6

8 oz "easy cook" rice	2 eggs
1 large onion (or 2 medium-sized)	1 heaped teaspoonful of Marmite
6 oz bacon (bacon bits are ideal)	2-3 tablespoons vegetable oil

Method

Boil the rice according to the instructions on the packet. Strain the rice through a colander and rinse it with very hot water to separate the grains. Leave the rice in the colander until required. Trim and cut the bacon into little pieces. Peel and slice the onion(s). Beat the 2 eggs. Dissolve the Marmite in a cupful of boiling water and stir well. Heat the oil in a very large frying pan and cook the bacon pieces in it, and then remove them from the pan. Next lightly fry the sliced onion(s) and then return the bacon bits to the pan. Mix the bacon and onions together and then slowly pour the beaten eggs over the mixture. Let the eggs cook very slowly, constantly stirring the mixture.

Start adding the cooked rice to the mixture and stirring well until all the oil has been absorbed. At this point add the cupful of Marmite to the pan, bringing the mixture back to the boil and then down to simmer. Keep adding the remainder of the rice to the mixture and stirring well. Mix it all up thoroughly. If the mixture is a little too wet it doesn't matter, just let it simmer gently until the excess moisture has evaporated. Serve piping hot with soy sauce (if liked).

With this recipe you can use up all sorts of leftovers or add other ingredients to your taste (e.g. mushrooms, mixed herbs etc.)

This recipe was given to my mother when she lived in Holland and it continues to be the favourite dish of all the Vordermans.

Cooking time: 45 minutes

"SMAKELIJK ETEN!"

Alexander III Monument
Postcard courtesy of Alan Barker

During a storm in 1286, King Alexander III set off from Edinburgh to be with his new wife, who was waiting for him at Kinghorn Castle. Reluctantly the ferryman set sail from Queensferry at the Royal command. In his haste the King ignored warnings that he should delay his journey and carried on. When Alexander had reached the cliffs just past Burntisland, his horse stumbled and the King fell to his death. The monument marks where he died.

Thai Spring Rolls

Pam McCaulay - Kirkcaldy

Ingredients - Serves 6

2 tablespoons plain flour
¼ pint water
2 oz dried rice vermicelli, broken into small pieces
1 garlic clove, crushed
1 green pepper, chopped finely
1 celery stick, chopped finely
2 spring onions, chopped finely
4 oz button mushrooms, sliced finely
2 teaspoons liquid seasoning, such as Maggi
½ teaspoon sugar
8 frozen spring roll sheets, 10 inches square, defrosted
oil for frying

Sauce:
4 tablespoons rice vinegar
4 tablespoons sugar
½ teaspoon salt
1 small red chilli, chopped finely

Method

To make the sauce, boil all the ingredients together. Stirring frequently until the sauce thickens. This will take about 5 minutes. Pour into a small bowl or saucer and set aside. Mix the flour and water together over a low heat, stirring constantly until thick and translucent. Pour into a saucer and set aside. Blanch the rice vermicelli in boiling water for 30 seconds. Stir and drain. Set aside.

Heat 1 tablespoon of the oil in a wok over a high heat. Add the garlic, green pepper, celery, spring onion and button mushrooms. Stir until the vegetables are softened. Add the liquid seasoning and sugar. Remove from the heat and transfer to paper towels to drain briefly. Stir in the rice vermicelli.

Cut the first spring roll sheet into 4 squares. Place about 2 teaspoons of the vermicelli mixture in the centre of each square. Fold 3 corners inwards like an envelope, and roll up the 4th corner. Dab a little of the flour and water paste on this corner to seal. At this stage the spring rolls can be chilled or frozen for use later.

Heat the oil in a wok until a light haze appears on top. Have ready a plate lined with paper towels. Deep-fry the spring rolls in batches until golden brown. Drain well on the paper towels.

Cooking time: 40 minutes

Peach and Tomato Salad

Ingredients - Serves 6

6 white peaches
6 large tomatoes
6 walnuts
6 leaves of basil

lemon juice
olive oil or walnut oil
salt and pepper

Method

Pour boiling water over the peaches and allow to stand for 30 seconds, depending on ripeness of fruit. Refresh in cold water and remove skin. Do the same with the tomatoes, they should be firm but full of flavour. Slice the tomatoes thinly and salt them, then cut the peaches into thin segments. Arrange both fruits in an overlapping circle, alternating the two. Squeeze the juice of a lemon over the salad and drizzle lightly with the oil (very lightly if using walnut oil instead of olive oil). Chop the walnuts and tear the basil leaves then scatter these over the salad. Mill some black pepper over and serve cold.

Cooking time: nil

Mums' Potato Cakes

Phillip Schofield - Actor, TV Personality

Ingredients - Serves 10

2 lb potatoes
milk and butter

salt and pepper
self-raising flour

Method

Boil potatoes until soft. Then drain and mash in the usual way with butter, milk and seasoning Add a little more butter so that the mixture is quite soft and creamy. Leave until almost cold, add the flour (about 1-1½ cupfuls or until mixture resembles a slightly stiff dough, it will be a little sticky). Take a portion of the mixture (about a sixth) and place on a well-floured board. Your hands will also need to have a lot of flour on them. Pat the mixture until flat and about ¾ inch thick. You can use a rolling pin, being very careful that the mixture doesn't stick to either the board or the rolling pin. Place the potato cakes on a large greased baking tray and bake in a moderately hot oven for 15-20 minutes or until golden brown. Eat straight away spread with a little butter.

Cooking time: 45 minutes

Zucchini Sticks and Sour Cream Dip

The Elephant & Castle Pub - Ottawa, Canada

Ingredients - Serves 4-6

4 zucchini (courgettes)
1 large egg, beaten
1 cup of milk
seasoned flour
hot oil to deep fry

Breadcrumbs:
6 slices of firm bread, crumbed
salt and pepper
ground oregano, thyme, and parsley
garlic powder

Method

Mix all breadcrumb ingredients together on a flat tray long enough to take the zucchini. Wash and dry zucchini and cut into finger size portions. Beat egg and milk together in a flat dish. Dip each zucchini finger in the flour and egg and repeat this process twice, then roll the zucchini finger in the breadcrumb mixture.

Deep fry until golden brown and drain on kitchen paper. Serve with sour cream and garlic dip or with your own favourite dip.

Cooking time: 20 minutes

Tomato Risotto

Helen MacDonald - Dental Surgeon, Burntisland

Ingredients - Serves 2-3

1 cup of long grain rice
1 small red or green pepper, finely chopped
1 dessertspoon concentrated tomato purée

1 small onion, finely chopped
1 tablespoon vegetable oil
pinch of herbs

Method

Cook the rice as per the instructions on the pack. When the rice is cooking, fry the onion and pepper in the oil gently taking care not to discolour it. Once the rice is cooked drain and return it to the saucepan and add the onion and pepper. Mix in the tomato purée and the herbs and stir thoroughly. Reheat and serve as a main course or an accompaniment to any meat dish.

Cooking time: 20 minutes

Creamy Baked Fennel

Ingredients - Serves 4

2 tablespoons lemon juice 2 oz butter
2 bulbs fennel, trimmed
4 oz low-fat soft cheese
¼ pint single cream
¼ pint milk
1 egg, beaten

2 teaspoons caraway seeds
2 oz fresh white breadcrumbs
salt and pepper
sprigs of parsley

Method

Preheat the oven to 180°C/350°F/gas mark 4

Bring a large saucepan of water to the boil and add the lemon juice. Slice the bulbs of fennel thinly and add them to the saucepan. Cook for 2-3 minutes to blanch, and then drain them well, and arrange in a buttered ovenproof baking dish. Beat the soft cheese in a bowl until smooth. Add the cream, milk and beaten egg, and whisk together until combined. Season with salt and pepper and pour over the fennel. Melt ½ oz of the butter in a small frying pan and fry the caraway seeds gently for 1-2 minutes, to release the flavour and aroma. Sprinkle over the fennel. Melt the remaining butter in a frying pan. Add the breadcrumbs and fry gently until lightly browned. Sprinkle evenly over the surface of the fennel. Bake for 25-30 minutes, or until the fennel is tender. Serve, garnished with sprigs of parsley

Cooking time: 50-60 minutes

Layered Aubergine, Potato and Tomato Casserole

Pam McCaulay - Kirkcaldy

Ingredients - Serves 6

2 medium aubergines
salt and freshly ground black pepper
9 small potatoes, peeled and sliced
2 large Spanish onions, chopped
6 tablespoons olive oil
2 garlic cloves, finely chopped

2 large green peppers, seeded and sliced
1 large red pepper, seeded and sliced
9-10 tablespoons chopped parsley
3 14 oz cans tomatoes
2 teaspoons paprika
3 tablespoons red wine vinegar

Method

Preheat the oven to 200°C/400°F/gas mark 6

Slice the aubergine very thinly, lay the slices on the draining board and sprinkle with salt. Leave to sweat for 30-40 minutes, then blot with absorbent kitchen paper. Cook the potatoes for 15 minutes in boiling salted water. Soften the onions in 4 tablespoons of oil over a low heat and add the garlic. Grease an earthenware casserole or dish (about 12 inches across and at least 3 inches deep) with oil. Make 3 layers of vegetables, starting with a third of the potato slices, then the peppers, cooked onion and garlic together with some of the pan oil, plus parsley. Add a can of tomatoes and their juice, squeezing the tomatoes through clenched fingers to break them up well. Season with salt, pepper and paprika and repeat until all ingredients are in the casserole. Sprinkle vinegar over the second layer and 1 tablespoon oil over the top of the dish. Cover with foil and bake in the oven for 1 hour. Then remove the foil, turn down the heat to 160°C/325°F/gas mark 3 and give it another 30-60 minutes to brown and concentrate the juices. Excellent hot or cold, this dish will also reheat well.

Cooking time: 2 hours

Tzatziki (Greek Cucumber and Yoghurt Dip)

Hazel Simpson - Heritage Trust Volunteer

Ingredients - Serves 4-6

2 cups plain yoghurt
2 large cucumbers
1 tablespoon minced garlic

1 tablespoon white vinegar
2 tablespoons olive oil
salt and pepper to taste

Method

Put yoghurt in a cheesecloth-lined sieve over a bowl. Drain several hours or overnight in the refrigerator. Peel, seed, and coarsely grate cucumbers. Drain well. Add garlic, vinegar, olive oil, salt, and pepper to cucumbers and mix well. Add drained yoghurt and blend. Serve with toast points, crackers, or pitta bread. Tzatziki is best made the day before to let the flavours blend together.

Cooking time: nil

The Parsonage
Sketch by courtesy of J M Peason

The Reverend George Hay Forbes was born in 1821 and was crippled from an early age. He studied logic, mathematics, Greek, Latin and French and also travelled extensively throughout Europe. He had an ear for languages; he could converse in twenty and had an overall knowledge of approximately fifty. He set himself the task of translating the book of Ecclesiastes into various languages. In order to carry out this task Forbes formed the Pitsligo Press in Burntisland and set the type for all his translations. He started his own school in the premises that are now occupied by the Inchview Hotel, but later transferred to the Parsonage when it was completed. He was also the Provost of Burntisland in 1896 but resigned due to a dispute over the building of the docks.

Indonesian Chestnut and Vegetable Stir-Fry with Peanut Sauce

Pam McCaulay - Kirkcaldy

Ingredients - Serves 4

Stir-fry:

3 tablespoon sesame oil
3-4 shallots, finely sliced
1 garlic clove, finely sliced
1-2 red chillies, deseeded and finely chopped
1 large carrot, cut into fine strips
1 courgette cut into fine strips
4 oz sugar snap peas, trimmed
3 inch piece of cucumber, cut into strips
8 oz oyster mushrooms, wiped and torn into small pieces, if large
1 yellow and 1 red pepper, de-seeded and cut into fine strips
8 oz canned whole peeled chestnuts, drained
2 tablespoon grated fresh root ginger finely grated
rind and juice of 1 lime
1 tablespoon chopped fresh coriander
salt and pepper
slices of lime to garnish

Sauce:

4 oz unsalted peanuts, roasted and ground
2 teaspoons hot chilli sauce
6 fl oz coconut milk
2 tablespoons soy sauce
1 tablespoon ground coriander
pinch of ground turmeric
1 tablespoon dark muscovado sugar

Method

To make the sauce, put all the ingredients into a small pan. Heat gently and simmer for 3-4 minutes. Heat the sesame oil in a wok. Add the shallots, garlic and chillies and stir-fry for 2 more minutes. Add the carrot, peppers, courgette and sugar snap peas to the wok and stir-fry for 2 more minutes. Add all the remaining ingredients to the wok and stir-fry briskly for about 5 minutes or until the vegetables are crisp, yet crunchy. Divide the stir-fry between 4 warmed serving plates and garnish with slices of lime. Serve with the peanut sauce.

Cooking time: 15 minutes

Crispy-Fried Vegetables with Hot and Sweet Dipping Sauce

Ingredients - Serves 4

vegetable oil, for deep-frying
1 lb selection of vegetables, such as cauliflower, broccoli, mushrooms, courgette, peppers and baby corn, cut into even sized pieces

Sauce:

6 tablespoons light malt vinegar
2 tablespoons Thai fish sauce or light soy sauce
2 tablespoons water
1 tablespoons soft brown sugar
pinch of salt
2 garlic cloves, crushed
2 teaspoons grated fresh root ginger
2 red chillies, de-seeded and chopped finely
2 tablespoons chopped fresh coriander

Batter:

4 oz plain flour
½ teaspoon salt
1 teaspoon caster sugar
1 teaspoon baking powder
3 tablespoons vegetable oil
7 fl oz warm water

Method

To make the batter, sift the flour, salt, sugar and baking powder into a large bowl. Add the oil and most of the water, then whisk together to make a smooth batter, adding extra water to give it the consistency of single cream. Chill for 20-30 minutes. Meanwhile, make the sauce. Heat the vinegar, fish sauce, water, sugar and salt until boiling. Remove from the heat and leave to cool. Mix together the garlic, ginger, chillies and coriander in a small serving bowl. Add the cooled vinegar mixture and stir together. Heat the vegetable oil for deep-frying in a wok. Dip the prepared vegetables in the batter and fry them, a few at a time, until crisp and golden. This will take about 2 minutes. Drain on paper towel. Serve the vegetables accompanied by the dipping sauce.

Cooking time: 30 minutes

Casserole of Wild Mushrooms

Kevin Woodford - Celebrity Chef, "Ready Steady Cook"

Ingredients - Serves 4

4 oz unsalted butter	pinch of paprika
2 tablespoons vegetable oil	2 tablespoons vermouth
2 oz shallots, finely chopped	2 teaspoons French mustard
2 garlic cloves, crushed	10 fl oz double cream
1 lb wild mushrooms, sliced	1 oz fresh Parmesan cheese, grated
2 tablespoons fresh coriander, chopped	salt and freshly ground black pepper
1 tablespoon chopped chives	

Method

Heat the butter and oil in a large frying pan; add the shallots and garlic then cook gently for 5 minutes. Add the mushrooms, coriander, chives and paprika, season with salt and pepper and cook over a medium heat for 1 minute until the mushrooms are golden. Pour in the vermouth, then stir in the mustard and cream. Mix thoroughly and bring to the boil. Check the seasoning and adjust if necessary. Serve straight away, sprinkled with Parmesan cheese.

Cooking time: 20 minutes

Stuffed Tomatoes

Ingredients - Serves 4

2 oz cracked wheat	2 tablespoons parsley, finely chopped
4 beefsteak tomatoes	2 tablespoons mint, finely chopped
1 courgette, finely chopped	1 tablespoon olive oil
3 cloves garlic, crushed	salt and ground black pepper
bunch spring onions, trimmed and finely chopped	

Method

Preheat the oven to 180°C/350°F/gas mark 4

Put the cracked wheat into a heatproof bowl and pour over enough boiling water to cover. Leave for 10 minutes. Meanwhile cut the tops off the tomatoes and scoop out the pulp with a spoon, leaving the outer case. Place half of the pulp into a sieve to drain over a bowl and leave the remainder aside. Chop the drained tomato pulp into small pieces and add the spring onion, courgette, garlic, parsley, mint and oil and mix well. Drain the cracked wheat and add to the vegetable ingredients. Season with salt and pepper and spoon the mixture into the tomato cases while still warm. Score the tomato shells with a sharp knife and place on a baking tray. Cook for 10 minutes until the tomatoes are heated through and the stuffing is hot. Serve as a main course or starter.

Cooking time: 15 minutes

Buffet Salad

Jane M. Maltman - Heritage Trust Volunteer

Ingredients - Serves 6-8

¼ pint double cream
2 red apples, cubed
4 oz Scottish Cheddar, cubed
4 oz cooked ham, cubed

small tin of peaches, cubed
2 oz salted peanuts
2 oz sultanas
1 lettuce

Method

Lightly whip the cream and mix in all the ingredients except the lettuce. Serve on a bed of lettuce and garnish with tomato and cucumber. Serve as part of a summer buffet
Cooking time: Nil

Steamed Jasmine Rice

Jeanne Rankin - Celebrity Chef, "Ready Steady Cook"

Serves 4-6

A general rule for cooking rice is to use equal volumes of rice and water. For example, 1 cup of rice, and 1 cup of water. Rinse the rice in plenty of cold water first, and drain well. Place in a heavy saucepan with the measured water. Add some salt, this is very individual, but a good pinch would do the above quantities. Bring to the boil and stir once. Cover and simmer for 10 minutes. Now turn off the heat, and make sure that the pot is covered tightly with a good lid or foil. Allow the rice to steam in its own heat for 20 minutes. Just before serving, fluff up with a fork.
Cooking time: 30 minutes

Baked Vegetables with Tomato Sauce

Costa and Jo Sofianos - A-Z Cleaning Services, Burntisland

Ingredients - Serves 5-6

2 lb potatoes
2-3 medium courgettes
2 medium aubergines
1 tin chopped tomatoes
2-3 green peppers

1 cup olive oil
2-3 onions
1 teaspoon mint, finely chopped
1 tablespoon parsley, chopped
salt and pepper

Method

Wash vegetables; remove the stalks from the courgettes and aubergines, and stalk and seeds from the peppers. Peel the potatoes and the onions. Cut all the vegetables into thick slices and place in an ovenproof dish. Add the tomatoes, parsley, mint and olive oil, salt and pepper and mix them well. Add a little warm water. Bake in a medium oven for 90 minutes. Serve warm as a first course with Feta cheese.
Cooking time: 1 hour 30 minutes

DESSERTS

Cromarty's Creme de la Creme Caramel

Cooking With Gas

Crivens!!

©Cluny & Cromarty MM

Exotic Fruit Brûlé

Ann McIntyre - Burntisland

Ingredients - Serves 4

3 egg yolks
¼ cup caster sugar
1 teaspoon vanilla essence
2-3 cups crème fraîche
2 teaspoons kirsch or brandy
1 small ripe mango peeled

1 small ripe pear peeled
1 large fig
8 large strawberries
freshly grated nutmeg
tuille biscuits to serve

Method

Preheat grill.

In a bowl beat egg yolks, sugar and vanilla essence together until pale, thick and creamy. Stir in crème fraîche and kirsch or brandy, set aside.

Remove mango stone and cut into thin slices, slice pear, fig and strawberries thinly. Arrange all the fruit over the bottom of 4 individual gratin dishes. Carefully pour one quarter of the custard mixture as evenly as possible onto each dish covering the fruit. Grate a little nutmeg over each custard.

Place on a tray and put under grill for 4-6 minutes or until custard is slightly caramelised.

Cool slightly and serve with a dusting of icing sugar and tuille biscuits.

Cooking time: 10 minutes

Pineapple Delight

Tib Simpson - Heritage Trust Volunteer

Ingredients - Serves 6

1 small packet of digestive biscuits, crushed
2 tablespoons syrup
6 oz butter
8 oz icing sugar

1 egg yolk
1 tin crushed pineapple
10 fl oz double cream
chocolate for decoration

Method

Melt 2 oz of the butter and syrup in a pan and add the crushed biscuits. Press into a greased tray.

Cream the rest of the butter with the icing sugar. Beat in the egg yolk and spread the mixture over the biscuit base. Whip cream (not too stiffly), add drained pineapple and spread on top. Refrigerate until set.

Before serving sprinkle with grated chocolate.

Cooking time: nil

Apricots under a Caramel Cloud

Ingredients - Serves 6

8 oz dried apricots, soak for 2 hours and drain
2 oz dark brown sugar
¾ pint water
8 oz cream cheese
6 oz caster sugar

½ pint soured cream
4 size 1 eggs separated
1 teaspoon vanilla essence
pinch of salt

Method

Preheat oven to 190°C/375°F/gas mark 5

Put apricots in a pan with sugar and water. Bring to the boil and simmer for 45 minutes. Remove lid and boil fiercely for a further 4 minutes until a light jam consistency. Spread on the base of a 9 inch ovenproof dish. Beat cream cheese with 4 oz caster sugar, gradually beat in the egg yolks, vanilla essence and the soured cream. Beat the 4 egg whites and salt until soft peak stage fold gently into cream mix and pour over the apricot base. Bake for 30 minutes until pale golden brown. Remove from oven and rest for 10 minutes (the dish will sink a little). Sprinkle with rest of caster sugar over the meringue and brown under a hot grill until caramelised. Chill in fridge before serving.

Cooking time: 1hour 20 minutes

Apricot Pastries

Aileen Braid - Heritage Trust Volunteer

Ingredients - Serves 6

15 oz can of apricots in syrup	8 oz white marzipan
3 sheets of ready rolled puff pastry	egg to glaze
flaked almonds	

Method

Preheat oven to 220°C/425°F/gas mark 7

Drain apricots in a sieve placed over a small pan, set apricots aside. Bring syrup to the boil and allow to simmer for 3 minutes until reduced and thickened. Remove from heat and allow to cool.

Cut each pastry sheet in half lengthways. Cut marzipan into 6 equal pieces flattening them until they are slightly smaller than the pastry. Place one piece of marzipan on each pastry sheet. Put two apricot halves in the centre of each piece of marzipan cut side down. Brush edges with egg and fold into an envelope, decoratively seal the edges, then place on a baking tray. Brush with syrup and sprinkle with flaked almonds. Bake in oven for 15-20 minutes until golden brown. Brush with glaze before serving.

Cooking time: 20 minutes

Spiced Fruit Brûlé

Aileen Braid - Heritage Trust Volunteer

Ingredients - Serves 4

1 large eating apple	1 teaspoon mixed spice
1 banana sliced	9 oz Marscapone cheese
1 oz sultanas	1 tablespoon milk
2 oz ready to eat dried apricots	2 oz soft brown sugar
grated rind and juice of half an orange	1 teaspoon cinnamon

Method

Preheat grill to medium. Peel, core and thinly slice the apple and place in a shallow 7 inch dish, along with sliced banana, apricot, sultanas, orange rind, juice and mixed spice. Beat together marscapone and milk until smooth, then spoon over the fruit. Smooth over the surface, sprinkle sugar and cinnamon over the top and place under a hot grill, cook for 6-8 minutes until top is golden brown and caramelised.

Cooking time: 10 minutes

Chocolate Mallow Ice Cream

Margaret Wilson - Mid Calder

Ingredients - Serves 6

2 oz chocolate (70% cocoa), grated
8 oz milk, scalded
16 mallows, cut into small pieces
¾ teaspoon salt, level
4 tablespoons granulated sugar

8 fl oz evaporated milk
1 tablespoon lemon juice
½ teaspoon ground cinnamon
cornflour for dusting

Method

Melt chocolate and add scalded milk to the bowl slowly, stirring constantly until thoroughly blended. Add mallows, sugar and salt. Place over a pan of hot water heating slowly, stirring constantly until mallows and sugar have dissolved. Chill. When cold, fold in whipped evaporated milk to which you have added lemon juice and cinnamon. Freeze for 3½ hours, beating the mixture every hour to break up the crystals and make ice cream smooth.

Cooking time: 30 minutes
Freezing time: 3 hours 30 minutes

Mississippi Mud Pie

Lyn Wolfendale - Godalming

Ingredients - Serves 8

8 oz marshmallows
1 lb plain chocolate
1 teaspoon instant coffee

8 fl oz double cream
4 oz hazelnuts, roasted and chopped
6 inch square tin

Method

Melt marshmallows and leave to cool. Melt chocolate and leave to cool. Whip cream to soft peak. Dissolve one tablespoon coffee in boiling water, leave to cool. Then stir chocolate and coffee into the marshmallows along with the nuts. Fold in whipped cream, spoon into prepared tin and smooth. Leave to chill overnight and cut into 1 inch fingers.

Cooking time: nil

Economical Cheesecake

Fiona Maltman-Shaw - Burntisland

Ingredients - Serves 6

2 oz margarine
4 oz digestive biscuits, crushed
½ pkt lemon jelly
½ cup water

½ cup caster sugar
1 small tin evaporated milk
3 oz soft cream cheese
1 teaspoon vanilla essence

Method

Melt margarine and add crushed biscuits. Line sponge tin with foil and press biscuit mixture into tin to form a base. Melt jelly in water and allow to cool. Whip evaporated milk and add sugar, cheese, essence and jelly. Pour into sponge tin over biscuit base. Put in fridge until set.

Cooking time: nil

Cranachan Ice Cream

Valerie Singleton - TV Presenter

Ingredients - Serves 6

1¾ pints of good quality vanilla ice cream
6 tablespoons runny honey
6 tablespoons whisky or whisky liqueur
2 oz butter

2 tablespoons brown sugar
2 oz pinhead oatmeal, toasted
fresh raspberries for decoration
oil for greasing

Method

Melt butter and sugar in a pan and bring to the boil. Mixture will form large bubbles on the surface when toffee stage has been reached. Stir continuously to avoid sticking. Add the pinhead oatmeal and turn out onto an oiled tray, and allow to cool. Break up the oatmeal praline into small pieces and reserve. Leave the ice cream at room temperature until soft. Warm honey until liquid, add the whisky then leave to cool slightly. Beat into the ice cream, then fold in the praline pieces and refreeze.

Serve in individual dishes decorated with a few fresh raspberries and any type of shortbread biscuit.

Cooking time: 10 minutes

Mini Muffins with Instant Ice Cream

Murren and Gavin McBride - Burntisland

Ingredients - Serves 4

1 oz butter, plus extra for greasing
a little sunflower oil for brushing
2 fl oz milk
1 egg, beaten
a few drops of vanilla extract
2 oz white chocolate
3 oz self raising flour
pinch of salt
½ teaspoon baking powder

1 oz light Muscovado sugar
2 tablespoons demerara sugar
½ oz macadamia nuts
8 fl oz double cream
2 tablespoons icing sugar,
   plus extra for dusting
11 oz frozen raspberries
mint sprigs to decorate

Method

Preheat the oven to 200°C/400°F/gas mark 6

Butter a 12-hole mini muffin tin generously with butter. Line a baking tray with foil and brush with oil. Melt the butter. Pour the milk into a bowl and whisk in the egg, butter and vanilla essence.

Chop the chocolate and set aside. Sift the flour, salt and baking powder into a bowl and stir in the muscovado sugar. Using a metal spoon, lightly fold in the milk mixture, taking care not to over mix. Stir in the chocolate and spoon into the muffin tins. Sprinkle with a little of the demerara sugar and bake for 10 minutes until well risen and firm.

Roughly chop the nuts. Place the remaining demerara sugar in a small saucepan with one tablespoon of water and cook gently until sugar dissolves. Stir in the nuts and continue cooking, once the mixture has started to caramelise pour out onto a greased tray and leave to cool. When set break the nut mixture into pieces. Put the cream, icing sugar and frozen raspberries, reserving a few for decoration, in a blender and mix on a low speed until combined. Shape the raspberry ice cream into scoops on a serving plate and sprinkle with nut mixture and add muffins to each plate. Decorate with the reserved raspberries and a sprig of mint and serve.

Cooking time: 30 minutes

Cranachan

Margaret Casey - Burntisland

Ingredients - Serves 6

1 pint double cream
3 tablespoons honey
3 tablespoons whisky

4 tablespoons thick plain yoghurt
1 oz fine oatmeal
6 oz raspberries

Method

Toast oatmeal until golden and allow it to cool.
Whip together cream, honey, and whisky until it forms peaks, and then fold in yoghurt. Spoon mixture into individual dishes and chill in fridge for 2-3 hours. Sprinkle with oatmeal and pile raspberries on top in the centre of the dishes. **Chilling time: 2-3 hours**

Summer Fruit Jelly

Anna Briggs - Burntisland

Ingredients - Serves 8

2 raspberry jellies, made with 1½ pints water
soft fruits e.g. raspberries, strawberries, blueberries
red or blackcurrants

juice of half a lemon
1 measure of Crème de Cassis

Method

Prepare fruit, cut large strawberries in half or quarters. Add lemon juice and cassis to jelly.
Arrange the fruit in layers in a large Pyrex® bowl, as it gives it a nice appearance. Pour half of the jelly mixture over the fruit. Cover the fruit with cling film and weigh down with a plate. Leave to set. When set remove plate and cling film, and pour the remaining jelly over the rest of the fruit. Leave to set again.
To serve, place bowl in a little warm water to slacken the jelly and invert onto a serving plate and dredge with caster sugar. **Cooking time: 5 minutes**

Apple Plate Pie

Anna Briggs - Burntisland

Ingredients - Serves 8

Pastry:
6 oz plain flour
3 oz margarine
pinch of salt
ground rice
1 tablespoon cold water to mix

Filling:
2 lb apples, roughly chopped
juice of half a lemon
4 oz light demerara sugar
½ teaspoon cinnamon
2 cardamom pods
1 teaspoon, water

Method

Preheat oven to 190°C/375°F/gas mark 5
Grease an 8-9 inch pie plate. Place apples, sugar, cinnamon, cardamom pods, lemon juice and water in a pan and simmer for 5 minutes. Allow to cool. Sift flour and salt into a bowl and rub in the margarine until mixture resembles breadcrumbs. Mix with cold water until pastry is bound together but not wet. Knead pastry a little, and then wrap in cling film and leave to rest in fridge.

Roll out one half of the pastry a little larger than the pie-plate. Lay on the pie-plate, brush pastry with beaten egg and sprinkle with ground rice. Put the apple filling on the pastry base, and brush edges with beaten egg. Roll out the remaining pastry so that it will cover the filling without stretching. Seal together and crimp the edges of the tart. Brush the surface with beaten egg and dredge with caster sugar. Bake in the middle of the oven at for 40 minutes until golden brown.

Cooking time: 40 minutes

The Erskine Church prior to the installation of the clock in 1930
Postcard courtesy of Alan Barker

Erskine Church Clock, Burntisland
Miss McOmish had a shock
When she died she left a clock
It chimes the quarter and the oor
For everyone both rich and poor
Anon.

Ginger, Almond and Fig Meringue

Dr. J. H. B. MacDonald - Burntisland, Erskine Church organist

Ingredients - Serves 6

4 oz whole almonds, blanched	4 egg whites
5 oz dried figs	8 oz caster sugar
3 oz preserved ginger	½ pint double cream

Method

Preheat the oven to 170ºC/325ºF/gas mark 3

Coarsely chop the almonds and toast them in the oven for 10 minutes. Chop the figs and ginger. Beat the egg whites until stiff, gradually adding the sugar, 2 tablespoons at a time, beating for 20 seconds between each addition. The resulting meringue should be stiff and glossy. Fold the dry ingredients into the meringue and spoon the mixture into an 8 inch cake tin with a removable collar. Bake the cake for 35 minutes or until a skewer comes out clean from the centre. Run a knife round the collar, and cool the cake. Whip the cream and spread it over the meringue. Chill it until you are ready to serve it.

Cooking time: 45 minutes

Japanese Toffee Apples
Pam McCaulay - Kirkcaldy

Ingredients - Serves 4

3 apples
1 tablespoon lemon juice
4 oz cornflour
2 tablespoons sesame seeds
¾ pint ground nut oil

4 oz ice cubes
l pint iced water
12 oz sugar
1 teaspoon vinegar

Method

Peel and core the apples and cut each into 6 pieces. Cut each piece into three. Sprinkle lemon juice over the apples immediately to prevent discolouration. Coat the apple pieces with cornflour and set them aside. Sauté the sesame seeds in a pan over a low heat. Set aside. Rub a serving plate with oil and set it aside. Place the ice cubes and iced water in a bowl and set them aside. Heat the oil and fry the apple for 10 minutes until nicely golden. Remove, drain and set aside. In another pan bring 350ml/l2 fl oz water to a vigorous boil. Add the sugar, stirring until it starts to caramelise, then add the vinegar and stir. Add the apple pieces until they are evenly coated with syrup. Sprinkle sesame seeds over the apple pieces and transfer them to a plate. Dip the syrup coated apple pieces into the iced water. Remove immediately or when the syrup hardens and becomes brittle.

It is worth practising this recipe a few times to achieve the correct contrast between the brittle, ice cold coating of caramelised sugar and the hot, tender apple centre.

Cooking time: 15 minutes

Soufflé au Grand Marnier
Ann McIntyre - Burntisland

Ingredients - Serves 4

2 tablespoons butter
2 tablespoons flour
½ pint hot milk
pinch of salt
5 egg yolks

4 tablespoons sugar
½ teaspoon vanilla extract
2 tablespoons Grand Marnier
6 egg whites

Method

Preheat oven to 170ºC/325ºF/gas mark 3

Melt the butter in the top of a double saucepan. Add the flour and cook, stirring, until well blended. Add the hot milk and salt. Cook the sauce, stirring constantly until smooth and thick. Continue cooking and stirring for a few more minutes. Let sauce cool slightly. Beat egg yolks with sugar and vanilla extract and mix well with the sauce. Stir in Grand Marnier.

Butter a soufflé dish. Beat the egg whites until stiff but not dry and fold into the cooled mixture. Pour into the prepared soufflé dish. Bake in the oven for 35 minutes or until soufflé is well risen and golden.

Cooking time: 45 minutes

Janice's Sticky Toffee Pudding
Starley Hall School, by Burntisland

Ingredients - Serves 6
6 oz chopped dates
2 oz butter
6 oz sugar
2 eggs
6 oz self-raising flour
½ teaspoon vanilla essence
1 level teaspoon baking powder

Sauce:
4 oz of muscovado sugar
.1 cup (5 fl oz) double cream
4 oz butter

Method
Preheat oven to 180°C/350°F/gas mark 4

Add the dates to a pan containing ½ pint water and the baking powder. Bring to the boil and cook until the dates are tender. Allow to cool. Cream the butter and sugar. Add the beaten eggs and the self-raising flour. Fold in the date mixture and mix well. Place mixture in a greased flan dish. Bake in oven for 45 minutes. After cooking cut into wedges and slightly separate them.

Sauce:
Put all ingredients in pan and stir until dissolved. Heat to boiling until caramelised (5-10 minutes). Pour sauce over wedges. When ready to serve, reheat in oven until warm. Serve with ice cream or cream or crème frâiche.

Delicious on its own or cold. **Cooking time: 55 minutes**

Hampden Place, now Cromwell Road, with St Serf's Episcopal Church on the left. The Church was built in 1905 and replaced the "Tin Church" that used to be on the site. The "Tin Church" was moved to Kinghorn and is still in use.
Houses have now been built on the field at the right hand side of the picture

Postcard Courtesy of Alan Barker

Cherry Cheese Cake
Alan Titchmarsh - Celebrity Gardener, "Ground Force"
"Good luck with the fund raising."

Ingredients - Serves 6
4 oz digestive biscuits
3 oz margarine
8 oz cream cheese
¾ cup icing sugar

dash vanilla essence
¼ pint double cream
1 tin cherry pie filling

Method
Crush biscuits and add to melted margarine to make base. Beat together cream cheese, icing sugar and vanilla essence. Whisk double cream until holding soft peaks and add to cream cheese mixture. Blend well and spoon onto biscuit base and chill until set. Spread the tin of cherry pie filling on top to complete the dish. **Cooking time: nil**

DESSERTS

Mimi's Blueberry Cheese Cake
Elephant & Castle Pub - Ottawa, Canada
Ingredients - Serves 12

Crust Base:
10 oz Digestive biscuit crumbs
3 oz melted butter
Topping:
2 cups frozen blueberries,
or raspberries
2 oz caster sugar
1 tablespoon cornflour

Cheese Filling:
13 oz soft cream cheese
5 oz caster sugar
2 large eggs
175 ml of sour cream
1 teaspoon vanilla essence
30 ml double cream
2 cups frozen blueberries

Method

Preheat oven to 170°C/325°F/gas mark 3

Grease and line an 8 x 2 inch spring form tin with greaseproof paper. Mix crumb mixture with melted butter and press into the bottom of the tin, then bake in the oven for 15 minutes. Leave to cool. Beat the cream cheese with the sugar and vanilla essence until well mixed, add the eggs one at a time and beat well again. Add the sour and double cream and incorporate it thoroughly.

Place 2 cups of defrosted blueberries on top of crumb base, and then pour the cheese mixture over the blueberries and the base. Bake in the centre shelf of the oven for 50 minutes or until set, but not brown. Leave to cool and set for a minimum of 6 hours. Finish cheesecake by placing half the blueberries for the glaze in a blender and blend until puréed. Place in a pan with the sugar and cornflour, and cook until clear. Add the remaining blueberries until soft but not broken. Cool mixture and spread on top of cheesecake. Leave to set before serving. **Cooking time: 1 hour 15 minutes**

Clootie Dumplin
Alistair Anderson - Burntisland
Ingredients - Serves 12

1 lb self-raising flour	½ lb currants	4oz candied peel (if desired)
1 teacup breadcrumbs, white or brown	¾ pound raisins	1 grated apple
1 teacup sugar	2-3 teaspoons cinnamon	milk to mix
1 teacup shredded suet	2-3 teaspoons ginger	large cloot (pudding cloth)

Method

Mix fruit, flour, sugar, breadcrumbs, suet and spices thoroughly. Add milk to make a fairly stiff consistency.

Preparing the cloot.
Scald the cloot, dust with flour then place the mixture in the centre. Bring the corners of the cloot together then tie securely with string leaving room for the pudding to swell (approximately a further third in volume). Boil steadily in plenty of water for 3-4 hours, topping up when necessary. Gently remove the cloot and place the dumpling on to a large plate. Place in front of a fire (preferably coal) and dry to form a skin, turning from time to time. If you don't have this luxury, a warm oven will suffice.

Serving suggestions.
Slice and serve while hot with custard or cream or eat cold as a cake. Can also be fried as part of a full Scottish breakfast. Sometimes when prepared for a special occasion silver thrupenny coins (sterilised) small charms or any currently available coin are added to the mix. This adds excitement to eating the dumpling but can be dangerous, especially with children, so warn everyone about the added ingredients.
Cooking time: 3-4 hours

Bread and Butter Pudding

Gary Rhodes - Celebrity Chef

"I wish you every success with the recipe book and your fund raising."

Ingredients - Serves 6-8

12 medium slices white bread, crusts cut off	8 egg yolks
50 g unsalted butter, softened	300 ml milk
1 vanilla pod or few drops of vanilla essence	25 g sultanas
300 ml double cream	25 g raisins
175 g caster sugar,	
plus extra for the caramelised topping	

Method

Requirement: 1.5-1.8 l pudding dish/basin, buttered.

Preheat the oven to 180°C/350°F/gas mark 4

Butter the bread. Split the vanilla pod and place in a saucepan with the cream and milk and bring to the boil. While it is heating, whisk together the egg yolks and caster sugar in a bowl. Allow the cream mix to cool a little, then strain it on to the egg yolks, stirring all the time. You now have the custard.

Cut the bread into triangular quarters or halves, and arrange in the dish in three layers, sprinkling the fruit between two layers and leaving the top clear. Now pour over the warm custard, lightly pressing the bread to help it soak in, and leave it to stand for at least 20-30 minutes before cooking to ensure that the bread absorbs all the custard. The pudding can be prepared to this stage several hours in advance and cooked when needed. Place the dish in a roasting tray three-quarters filled with warm water and bake for 20-30 minutes until the pudding begins to set. Don't overcook it or the custard will scramble. Remove the pudding from the water bath; sprinkle it liberally with caster sugar and glaze under the grill on a medium heat or with a gas gun to a crunchy golden finish. When glazing, the sugar dissolves and caramelises, and you may find that the corners of the bread begin to burn. This helps the flavour, giving a bittersweet taste that mellows when it is eaten with the rich custard, which seeps out of the wonderful bread sponge when you cut into it.

Cooking time: 20-30 minutes

Burntisland Fair
Postcard courtesy of Alan Barker

When James V made Burntisland a Royal Burgh in 1541 he granted the town certain priviledges. These included the right to hold a twice weekly market and "a common fair once a year on the feasts of Saints Peter and Paul". This fair, held on the 29th June, was the only time when merchants from outside the burgh were allowed to sell manufactured goods within the town.

Charles I later granted the town two fairs in June and November, each lasting 8 days. By 1815 the fair had moved to the 10th July and today extends over the summer months.

Rhubarb Pie

Kirsty Wark - TV Presenter

Ingredients - Serves 6

Pastry:
6 oz plain flour
4 oz self-raising flour
2 oz ground almonds
6 oz castor sugar
1 egg, beaten with milk and juice of 1/2 lemon
6 oz butter

Filling:
½ lb new season rhubarb
4 tablespoons strawberry jam or:
2 tablespoons jam and 4 oz fresh strawberries

Method

Preheat oven to 190°C/375°F/gas mark 5

Sift plain and self-raising flour in a bowl, rub in butter until the mixture looks like breadcrumbs. Mix in sugar and the ground almonds then bind together with egg and lemon juice. Knead lightly and chill for 15 minutes in fridge.

Combine rhubarb and strawberries/jam and place in the bottom of a pie dish. Roll out pastry and cover filling, brush with a little beaten egg and bake in a hot oven until golden brown.

Cooking time: 35-40 minutes

Black Forest Trifle

Cilla Black - TV Personality, "Blind Date"

Ingredients - Serves 8

sponge cake, or any stale cake
tin of pitted cherries
glacé cherries for decoration
custard powder
chocolate flake or apple crunch breakfast cereal

black cherry jelly
cherry brandy
glacé cherries
double cream

Method

Line the base of the trifle bowl with sponge cake (or stale cake) soaked in the juice from the tin of cherries together with a good dash of cherry brandy (or sherry). Make the black cherry jelly, pour on the top of the sponge cake, mix in the pitted cherries and allow to set.

Make the thick custard with the custard powder, or for real luxury make an egg custard, pour on top of the jelly. When custard has cooled, whisk up the double cream and pipe on top. Sprinkle with chocolate flake and decorate with glacé cherries.

Serve when completely set.

Cooking time: 20 minutes

Iced Lemon Parfait

David S.Wilson - Master Chef, Peat Inn

Ingredients - Serves 8

6 eggs
6 egg yolks
strained juice of 2 lemons
grated zest of 2 lemons

3 sheets of leaf gelatine
½ pint double cream
7 oz sifted icing sugar

Method

Required: Terrine 11 x 4 x 3 inch deep

Soften gelatine in cold water. In bowl of mixer, whip eggs, egg yolks, sifted sugar and lemon zest until mixture is pale in colour and frothy. Warm lemon juice. Squeeze out softened gelatine, add to warm lemon juice and stir until dissolved. Whip in the gelatine/lemon mixture to the egg mixture, then whip in the cream. Line the terrine with cling film then pour mixture in. Cover and freeze.

Cooking time: nil

Boozy Bread and Butter Bake

Alex and Maggie MacDonald - Burntisland Heritage Trustees

"Our thanks to the Scotch Whisky Heritage Centre for this recipe. It is a wonderful blend of continental, tropical and Scottish ingredients".

Ingredients - Serves 6-10

1 pint double cream	8 large croissants
6 medium egg yolks	2 oz butter
4 oz white chocolate	2 oz pressed dates, coarsely chopped
generous measure of whisky	

Method

Preheat oven to 190°C/375°F/gas mark 5

Using a heavy-based pan, warm the cream gently. Break up the chocolate and add it to the cream. Stir gently to mix in the melting chocolate, taking care not to let it burn.

Meanwhile, cut the croissants vertically into three or four slices. Arrange in a buttered ovenproof dish then scatter the chopped dates on top. Melt the butter and pour evenly over the surface of the croissants. Beat the egg yolks, and add the warm cream to the yolks. Stir in the whisky, and then pour the egg and cream mixture over the croissants. Bake for 30-35 minutes or until the mixture is set and lightly browned. Serve piping hot with single cream and a little bit more of the cratur (whisky) on the side.

Cooking time: 45 minutes

Banoffee Pie

Carol Smillie - TV Presenter

Ingredients - Serves 12

1 large packet of digestive biscuits	10-12 bananas
½ lb melted unsalted butter	1½ pints of double cream
½ teaspoon dried ginger	2 oz castor sugar
1 tin condensed milk	1 oz dark chocolate

Method

Boil the unopened tin of condensed milk in a pan of water for 2½ hours and leave to cool down for at least 6 hours before opening.

Note: Do not allow water to boil dry, as the tin will explode.

Place biscuits into a food processor and grind until crumbed. Add dried ginger and then slowly add melted butter. Place the mixture into a loose-bottomed flan dish and press firm. Allow to set in the fridge for approximately 30 minutes. Open the tin of condensed milk carefully. This will be set. Now spread onto the biscuit base. Slice bananas and spread evenly over the toffee (use your judgement as to the quantity). Whip up the double cream with the caster sugar and pipe all over the bananas. Grate the dark chocolate over the cream and put in the fridge until ready to serve.

Cooking time: 2 hours 30 minutes

Tiramisu
Kevin Woodford - Celebrity Chef, "Ready Steady Cook"

Ingredients - Serves 6

4 egg yolks
2 oz caster sugar
6 oz marscapone cheese grated
10 fl oz freshly made black coffee
4 tablespoons brandy

2 tablespoons rum
36 boudoir biscuits
4 oz good quality plain chocolate,
3 tablespoons chopped mixed nuts

Method

Whisk the egg yolks and caster sugar together until pale and creamy; the mixture should be thick enough to leave a trail on the surface when drizzled from the whisk. Fold in the marscapone cheese. Mix the coffee with the brandy and the rum and dip the biscuits into it to just moisten them.
Cover the base of a serving dish with a layer of the soaked biscuits and then spread some of the marscapone mixture on top. Sprinkle with some of the grated chocolate. Repeat the layers until all the ingredients have been used. Chill the tiramisu overnight and then decorate with the chopped nuts before serving.
Cooking time: nil

Apple and Rhubarb Crumble
Rt. Hon. Gordon Brown, MP - Chancellor of the Exchequer

Ingredients - Serves 4

6 oz flour (mixture of brown and white flour is best)
3 tablespoons extra brown sugar
8 oz rhubarb cut into small chunks
8 oz cooking apples, peeled and cored and cut into chunks

2 oz low fat margarine
2 oz butter
2 oz soft brown sugar

Method

Preheat oven to 200°C/400°F/gas mark 6
Put flour, margarine and butter in a large mixing bowl and rub the fat into the flour until it resembles fine breadcrumbs. I have found that you need half margarine/half butter to combine good health with good taste. Stir in 2 oz sugar. Put the rhubarb and apple into a pie dish. Sprinkle 3 tablespoons of sugar and a dash of water over the fruit. Pile the crumble mixture over the fruit and smooth over the surface pressing it down a little. Bake in the oven for 25-30 minutes until golden and bubbling.
Serve the crumble with custard, yoghurt or ice cream. If you have any left over it is also good cold the next day. In the summer it can be made with apple and blackberry or raspberry.
Cooking time: 25-30 minutes

Quick Butterscotch Sauce
Irene McCafferty - Burntisland

Ingredients - Serves 4

3 oz caster sugar
3 oz syrup
½ teaspoon lemon juice

1 oz butter
3 fl oz double cream
1 egg yolk, beaten

Method

Boil together in a pan the sugar, syrup, lemon juice and the butter until the consistency is like jam. Test in the same way. Pour a little onto a saucer and if the surface wrinkles when it is tipped on its side the mixture is ready. Beat the egg yolk with the cream and fold into the mixture. Pour into a serving jug and use as a topping for ice creams.

Cooking time: 20 minutes

Microwave Dumpling

Helen Frier - Heritage Trust Volunteer

Ingredients - Serves 6-8

1 cup of water	1 teaspoon cinnamon
½ lb margarine	1 teaspoon baking powder
1 cup caster sugar	1 lb plain flour
1 lb dried fruit	1 tablespoon dark treacle
1 teaspoon mixed spice	2 eggs

Method

Grease a 3 pint microwave bowl, and line with greaseproof paper.

Place water, sugar, margarine, dried fruit, treacle, and all the spices into a pot and heat until margarine melts. Simmer for one minute, then remove from heat. Mix in flour, baking powder and eggs. Pour mixture into the lined bowl and cook on high for 9-10 minutes until firm to the touch.

Cooking time: 11 minutes

Mocha Mallow Cream

Ingredients - Serves 4

8 oz marshmallows	1 tablespoon of whisky cream liqueur
1 tablespoon instant coffee	1 oz chopped walnuts
¼ pint double cream, whipped	⅓ pint milk

Method

Put mallows, milk and coffee in a bowl. Dissolve over a pan of hot water and allow to cool. Add the liqueur when mixture is beginning to set. Fold in half the cream and half the chopped nuts. When mixture is set decorate with the remaining cream and chopped nuts.

Cooking time: 10 minutes

Fruit and Cream

Ishbel Mitchell - Heritage Trust Volunteer

Ingredients - Serves 2

1-2 nectarines, sliced	4 oz strawberries
1 small bunch of seedless grapes	2 tablespoons of kirsch
1 macaroon or 3-4 ratafia or amaretti biscuits, broken into small pieces	1 small tub of crème fraîche
	2 tablespoons of soft muscovado sugar

Method

Hull the strawberries and halve them, if large. Divide the fruit into two glass serving dishes and add the broken biscuits. Pour the kirsch onto the biscuits, then spoon the crème fraîche over the fruit. Scatter the surface with the sugar to give a good even cover. Leave in the fridge, preferably overnight. The sugar will melt and leave the surface with a caramel sauce. Serve straight from the fridge.

Preparation time: 20 minutes

Sticky Toffee Bread Pudding

Janet Barr - Glenrothes

Ingredients - Serves 4

175 g butter
4 tablespoons syrup
150 g brown sugar

¾ pint double cream
100 g pecan nuts
400 g cinnamon bread, sliced and cut into triangles

Method

Place butter, syrup and sugar in a saucepan, then melt gently until dissolved. Bring to the boil and cook rapidly for 4 minutes. Dip bread in cream and layer in a greased ovenproof dish, and then sprinkle over some of the nuts. Pour over some sauce and repeat until all ingredients are used up. Bake in a hot oven for 15-20 minutes.

Cooking time: 35 minutes

Curd Cheese Tart

Revd. Canon Valerie Nellist - St. Serf's Church, Burntisland

"Best wishes for the project."

Ingredients - Serves 6

1 egg
1 tablespoon sugar
½ lb curds (cottage cheese will do)
a few raisins, currants or sultanas

½ oz butter, melted
grated nutmeg, to taste
short crust pastry to line a 7inch flan dish or similar utensil

Method

Preheat oven to 220ºC/425ºF/gas mark 7
Line the flan dish or tin with the pastry. Whip the egg; add the sugar, curds, dry fruit, melted butter and grated nutmeg. Pour the mixture into the pastry case. Bake in the hot oven for about 25 minutes.

Cooking time: 25 minutes

Hot Fudge Sauce

Michael Barrymore - Comedian and TV Presenter

Ingredients - Serves 4

3 oz soft brown sugar
2 level tablespoons golden syrup
1 oz margarine
4 tablespoons unsweetened evaporated milk

Method

Place all the ingredients in a small strong saucepan and heat gently for about 5 minutes stirring until they are well blended together. Do not allow mixture to boil.
Serve on top of ice cream, straight from the pan.
This recipe for hot fudge sauce is wonderful when poured over ice cream, or as a sauce for banana split!

Cooking time: 5 minutes

Marble Cake

Miss Peggy Dick - Burntisland

Ingredients - Serves 8

4 oz butter or margarine
4 oz caster sugar
2 eggs
5 oz self-raising flour, sifted

pinch of salt
½ teaspoon vanilla essence
2 tablespoons milk
1 tablespoon cocoa, rounded

Method

Preheat oven to 190°C/375°F/gas mark 5
Required: 1 lb loaf tin
Cream the butter and sugar until light. Beat in the eggs one at a time; (if the mixture starts to separate add a little of the flour). Add half the flour, salt and the vanilla essence. Divide the mixture in half. To one half of the mixture add the cocoa powder and mix well. Alternate spoonfuls of the two mixtures side by side in greased and floured tin (6-7 inches). Level and bake for 45-50 minutes in a moderate oven. When cool decorate with chocolate butter icing.
Cooking time: 50 minutes

Hanover Biscuits

Miss Peggy Dick - Burntisland

Ingredients - Serves 12

4 oz butter
3 oz caster sugar
8 oz self-raising flour

1 egg (separated)
pinch of salt

Method

Preheat oven to 190°C/375°F/gas mark 5
Cream the butter and sugar. Add the egg yolk and half the white, gradually mixing in all the sifted flour and salt. Roll out very thinly and cut into approximately 12 rounds and bake on a greased baking sheet for 10 minutes. Sandwich together with jam while still warm, leave to cool.
When cold, mix enough icing sugar into the remaining egg white to give a coating consistency and ice each biscuit. Leave to set.
Cooking time: 10 minutes

Perkins

Christine Dewar - Burntisland Community Award Winner 1988

Ingredients - Serves 12

2 teacups of self-raising flour
1 teacup porridge oats
1 teacup of sugar
1 teaspoon ginger
1 teaspoon mixed spice

1 teaspoon cinnamon
1½ teaspoons baking soda
1 tablespoon syrup
¼ lb butter
1 egg

Method

Preheat oven to 180°C/350°F/gas mark 4
Mix all dry ingredients together. Melt butter and syrup. Mix all the ingredients together and then add the egg. Form into small balls and place on greased baking sheet. Bake for 15 minutes. When baked place on wire tray to cool.
Cooking time: 15 minutes

Black Bun

Bob Fairley - Heritage Trust Volunteer

Ingredients - Serves 10

Pastry:
6 oz butter
8 oz self-raising flour
pinch of salt
1 size 3 egg, beaten
a little cold water
pinch of black pepper
1 teaspoon ground ginger
¼ pint milk

Filling:
8 oz self-raising flour
4 oz sugar
1 lb raisins
1 lb currants
2 oz mixed peel
2 oz blanched almonds
1 teaspoon cinnamon

Method

Preheat oven to 150°C/300°F/gas mark 2
Required: 8 inch round cake tin
To make the pastry, rub the fat into the flour and salt and mix with some of the beaten egg and sufficient cold water to make a stiff paste. Roll out about two thirds of the pastry and use to line the greased cake tin. Roll out the remaining third to a round shape to cover the filling.
To make the filling, Mix the flour and the remaining ingredients. The mixture should be barely moist. Put the mixture into the lined baking tin and cover with the remaining pastry. Seal around the edges and brush all over with the remaining egg. Bake for 2½ hours
Store in an airtight tin till used.
Cooking time: 2 hours 30 minutes

Baths and Tea Rooms.
Now a private house.
Postcard Courtesy of Alan Barker

Tattie Scones

Alistair Anderson - Burntisland

Ingredients - Serves 8

½ lb cold mashed potato
½ oz butter

2 oz plain flour
salt to taste

Method

Preheat oiled griddle.
Mash potatoes, butter and salt together; mix in flour until the paste will not take any more. Roll very thin, cut out by hand into squares and diagonally across into triangles. Prick surface with a fork and cook on griddle for 3 minutes on each side. Serve warm and buttered. **Cooking time: 6 minutes**

Parlies (Scottish Parliament Cakes)

Margaret Casey - Burntisland

Ingredients - Serves 10

8 oz plain flour

4 oz margarine

2 oz caster sugar

2 tablespoons treacle or golden syrup

1 teaspoon ground ginger (optional)

1 egg

Method

Preheat oven to 180°C/350°F/gas mark 4

Grease baking tray. Cream butter and sugar, add the egg and flour then mix well. Drop dessertspoonfuls of the mixture onto the baking tray and leave to expand. Bake for 15-20 minutes until golden brown. Place on a wire rack to cool.

Cooking time: 15-20 minutes

Chocolate Triangles

Josie Brown - Burntisland

Ingredients - Serves 20

3 oz butter

5 oz plain chocolate

1 can condensed milk

10 oz Digestive biscuits, crushed

1 oz raisins

white chocolate for decoration

Method

Required: 7 x 11 inch baking tray

Put chocolate, butter and condensed milk in a pan and heat gently until melted. Add the crushed biscuits and raisins. Stir well. Press mixture into the baking tray that has been lined with tin foil. Chill until firm. Cut into triangles and decorate with melted white chocolate by drizzling it in a zigzag fashion over the chocolate triangles.

Cooking time: 5 minutes

Upland Biscuits

Marion and Robert Gray - Carmatters, Kirkcaldy

Ingredients - Serves 10

8 oz margarine

5 oz caster sugar

10 oz self-raising flour

2 oz custard powder

1 large egg, beaten

pinch of salt

Method

Preheat oven to 180°C/350°F/gas mark 4

Cream margarine and sugar until soft then add the beaten egg then the rest of ingredients. Knead well and roll out and cut with a small cutter. Bake for 10 minutes until pale brown. When cold, sandwich together in pairs with jam. Decorate with a little glacé icing.

Cooking time: 10 minutes

Banana Loaf

Mrs Porteous - Burntisland

Ingredients - Serves 8

8 oz self-raising flour
3 small ripe bananas
1½ oz margarine, melted

1 egg
4½ oz caster sugar

Method

Preheat oven to 150°C/300°F/gas mark 2
Required: 1 lb loaf tin
Mash bananas, put all the remaining ingredients into a bowl and mix together. Pour into a greased loaf tin and bake for 1 hour. Cool on a wire rack.
Cooking time: 1 hour

Rossend Castle (formerly Burntisland Castle)
Postcard Courtesy of Alan Barker

Mary, Queen of Scots visited Burntisland Castle in February 1563. It was made notable by the French poet Chastellard who was discovered hiding in her bedchamber. The Queen's maids raised the alarm, and as this was the second time he had breached the royal bedchamber, Chastellard was subsequently tried and executed at St. Andrews on the 22nd February 1563.

Guinness Cake

Agnes McGregor - Kirkcaldy

Ingredients - Serves 8

10 oz self-raising flour
½ lb margarine
4 eggs

8 oz brown sugar
1 lb dried mixed fruit
¼ pint Guinness

Method

Preheat oven to 140°C/275°F/gas mark 1
Cream sugar and margarine. Add eggs. Fold in flour and fruit. Stir in two tablespoons of Guinness. Bake in oven for approximately 2 hours. Cool slightly, then gently pour remaining Guinness over cake. Best kept for a week before eating.
Cooking time: 2 hours

Zucchini Bread

Wendy Hurley - New Jersey, USA

Ingredients - Serves 16

3 large zucchini (courgettes)
½ cup walnuts
3 eggs
1 cup vegetable oil
1½ cups sugar

3 cups flour, plain
1 teaspoon salt
1 teaspoon baking soda
2 teaspoons baking powder
3 teaspoons cinnamon

Method

Preheat the oven to 180ºC/350ºF/gas mark 4
You will need a food processor (or do it by hand) and two loaf pans 9 x 5 inch.
Using a processor-shredding blade, process the zucchini. Place in a colander, sprinkle lightly with salt and let it drain while preparing the other ingredients. Using the steel blade, chop the walnuts coarsely and set aside. Continue with the steel blade and combine eggs, oil and sugar. Sift the flour, salt, baking soda, baking powder and cinnamon. Add one cup of dry ingredients at a time to the processor. Blend until just combined. When all dry ingredients have been added, fold in the zucchini and walnuts with a spoon. Pour into the loaf pans. Bake for one hour or until a skewer inserted in the middle comes out clean. Cool the loaves in the pans on a rack. Remove when cool and wrap in foil.
This bread is suitable for freezing.
Cooking time: 1 hour

Microwave Bran Muffins

Jean Campden - Burntisland

Ingredients - Serves 8

3 tablespoons milk
1 egg
2 oz whole bran cereal
2 tablespoons oil
2 oz raisins

2 oz treacle
3 oz self-raising flour
¼ teaspoon bicarbonate of soda
¼ teaspoon ground cinnamon
¼ teaspoon salt

Method

Beat milk and egg together then stir in bran cereal, leave to stand for 1 minute. Stir in the oil, raisins and the treacle. Add the dry ingredients and stir until they are moistened. Spoon the batter mixture into microwave custard cups that have been lined with muffin cases. Cook four at a time in the microwave on high for 3 minutes or according to the oven output. Leave to cool.
For gluten free version, substitute self-raising flour and bran cereal with gluten free flour, plus 1 teaspoon of baking powder and 2 oz cooked rice.
Cooking time: 15 minutes

Cherry and Coconut Slice

Doreen Thomas - Burntisland

Ingredients - Serves 12

10½ oz self-raising flour
6½ oz soft light brown sugar
4½ oz butter
6 oz chopped glacé cherries

1 egg, beaten
4½ oz desiccated coconut
5 fl oz milk

Method

Preheat oven to 180°C/350°F/gas mark 4

Combine flour, sugar and butter; rub to a crumbly mixture. Divide the mixture in half. Press one half firmly into the bottom of a well greased oblong tin 12 x 10 x 1 inch. Add cherries, beaten egg and milk to the rest of the mixture, pour on to the base and sprinkle with the desiccated coconut. Bake in the oven for 30 minutes. Cut into squares whilst still warm.

Cooking time: 30 minutes

Smiddy Loaf

Mike Japp - Heritage Diver

"This is my mother's old recipe for a tea loaf called Smiddy Loaf which she has passed on to us. It's great when just about cooled off from the oven with melted butter."

Ingredients - Serves 6-8

4 oz margarine	8 oz sultanas	**Add:**
2 teaspoons mixed spice	1 teacup sugar	2 teacups plain flour
1 teacup boiling water	1 small teaspoon of baking soda	2 eggs
pinch of salt		1 teaspoon baking powder

Method

Preheat oven to 180°C/350°F/gas mark 4

Boil the above in a large pan for 5 minutes and set aside to cool. Add 2 teacups of plain flour, 2 eggs and one teaspoon of baking powder. Mix well. Bake in a greased 2 lb loaf tin in a moderate oven for 1½ hours.

Cooking time: 1 hour 30 minutes

Date and Banana Loaf

Alexina McGregor Baird - Norwich

Ingredients - Serves 8

8 oz self-raising flour	1 large banana
pinch of salt	4 oz chopped dates
4 oz margarine	1 large beaten egg
4 oz caster sugar	4 tablespoons of milk

Topping:

½ oz chopped walnuts
2 teaspoons demerara sugar
1 tablespoon coffee essence

Method

Preheat oven to 180°C/350°F/gas mark 4

Required: 7 oz cake tin

Sift flour and salt into a bowl. Rub in margarine. Stir in sugar and dates. Mash banana with beaten egg and milk. Stir in liquid and beat until smooth. Bake in oven for 45-60 minutes. Mix all the topping ingredients together and spread over the top of the loaf and bake for further 15 minutes.

Cooking time: 1hour 15 minutes

Austrian Apple and Almond Cake

Susan Muir - Burntisland

Ingredients - Serves 8

5 oz butter
2 large eggs, beaten
8 oz caster sugar
1 teaspoon almond essence

8 oz self-raising flour.
1½ level teaspoon baking powder
1½ lb apples, Golden Delicious are best
icing sugar for dusting

Method

Preheat oven to 170°C/325°F/gas mark 3

Required: 8 or 9 inch loose bottomed or springform tin greased with butter.

Melt the butter until it is just runny but not too warm. Pour into a large bowl. Add the beaten eggs, sugar and almond essence. Beat well until mixed. Sift the flour with the baking powder and then fold into the mixture with a metal spoon. Spread two-thirds of the mixture in the cake tin. Place the peeled and thinly sliced apples on top. Spread the remaining cake mixture on top of the apples. Bake the cake for about 1½ hours. Leave to cool slightly in the tin before running a knife around the edge of the cake and loosening the bottom. Dust with icing sugar when cool.

Note: If this cake is baked in a 9 inch tin it seems more like an Austrian Torte and less like an English teatime cake. It also makes it more suitable to serve as a dessert with cream.

There appears to be not quite enough mixture to cover the apples when using a 9 inch tin but it doesn't matter because it all melts down and the apples look nice sticking out of the top. It only needs to cook for 1 hour because it will not be so deep.

Cooking time: 1hour 30 minutes

Dot's Christmas Cake

Dorothy Archibald - Burntisland

Ingredients - Serves a whole family

9 oz plain flour
½ level teaspoon salt
1 level teaspoon cinnamon
1 rounded teaspoon mixed spice
½ level teaspoon powdered nutmeg
1 lb seedless raisins
1 lb sultanas
12 oz currants

3 tablespoons brandy
4 oz chopped, candied peel
4 oz glacé cherries
4 oz blanched, flaked almonds
8 oz butter
8 oz soft brown sugar
6 eggs

Method

Preheat oven at 190°C/375°F/gas mark 5

Required: 8-9 inch cake tin.

Cream butter and sugar until fluffy. Beat eggs and add gradually to butter and sugar. Add all dry ingredients. Chop cherries and almonds and add to mixture. Line the cake tin with greaseproof paper and turn in mixture. Bake 1½ hours then reduce heat to 150°C/300°F/gas mark 2 for a further 1½-2 hours. Allow cake to cool before removing from tin. Prick base of cake and add brandy or rum. Store in airtight tin until ready for use. Decorate as required.

Cooking time: 3-3½ hours

The Docks
Postcard courtesy of Alan Barker

Burntisland has been a busy port for the last 500years. It is a natural seaport and the locals have made their living by fishing shipping and shipbuilding. Around 1793, for 10 years, Burntisland had a thriving herring fleet until stocks diminished.
On the 1st March 1850 the first rail ferry in the world sailed from Granton to Burntisland. This meant a whole goods train could cross the Forth in about 40 minutes. This ferry traffic provided work for local people as porters, dock labourers and railway workers. The ferries plied their trade until the rail link was completed to the South via the Forth Rail Bridge in 1890.

All-in-One Chocolate Sponge
The Rt. Hon. Tony Blair, MP - Prime Minister
"This recipe is sent with best wishes."

Ingredients - Serves 8

110 g self-raising flour (sifted)
1 teaspoon baking powder
110 g soft margarine, at room temperature

110 g caster sugar
2 large eggs
1 tablespoon cocoa powder

To finish:
icing sugar
jam and/or fresh cream

Method

Preheat the oven to 170°C/325°F/gas mark 3
Required: Two 18 cm sponge tins, no less than 4 cm deep, lightly greased and lined with greaseproof paper (also greased) or silicone paper.
Take a large roomy mixing bowl and sift flour and baking powder into it, holding the sieve high to give the flour a good airing. Then simply add all the other ingredients to the bowl and whisk them, preferably with an electric hand whisk, till thoroughly combined. If the mixture doesn't drop off a wooden spoon easily when tapped on the side of the bowl, then add 1 or 2 teaspoons of tap-warm water, and whisk again. Now divide the mixture between the two prepared tins, level off and bake on the centre shelf of the oven for about 30 minutes.
When cooked leave them in the tins for only about 30 seconds, then loosen the edges by sliding a palette knife all round and turn them out onto a wire cooling rack. Peel off the base papers carefully and when cool, sandwich them together with jam or lemon curd (or jam and fresh cream) and dust with icing sugar.
Cooking time: 30 minutes

Banana and Walnut Loaf

Sue Nicholls - Actress, "Audrey Roberts in Coronation Street"

"Lots of love and sincere best wishes".

Ingredients - Serves 8

4 oz margarine
6 oz soft light brown sugar
2 eggs
2 ripe bananas, mashed

8 oz self raising flour
1 teaspoon baking powder
1 teaspoon ground mixed spice
2 oz walnuts

Topping:
1 banana, sliced and dipped in lemon juice
2 tablespoons clear honey

Method

Preheat oven to 180°C/350°F/gas mark 4
Required: 2 lb loaf tin
Cream together the margarine and sugar until light and fluffy. Gradually beat in the eggs and bananas. Sieve the flour, baking powder and mixed spice and fold in lightly. Stir in the walnuts. Spoon the mixture into the greased and lined loaf tin. Bake in a preheated oven for 50-55 minutes until well risen and golden. Cool on a wire rack. When cold, decorate with sliced bananas and brush with honey.
Cooking time: 50-55 minutes

Florentines

Lyn Wolfendale - Godalming

Ingredients - Portions 15

2 oz butter
2 oz flour
2 oz sugar
1 tablespoon clear honey
extra butter for greasing

2 oz glacé cherries, chopped
1 oz mixed candied peel
1 oz almonds, chopped
4 oz plain chocolate
extra flour for dusting

Method

Preheat oven to 180°C/350°F/gas mark 4
Grease two baking sheets, sprinkle with flour then shake off any excess. Put butter sugar and honey in a pan and melt slowly. Remove from the heat and stir in the flour, cherries, candied peel and chopped almonds. Drop spoonfuls of the mixture onto the baking sheets and flatten out slightly, leaving enough room for them to spread during cooking. Bake for about 10 minutes or until brown and crisp. Cool on a wire rack. Melt chocolate in a small bowl over a pan of simmering water. Spread over the bottom of the Florentines. When the chocolate is nearly set, mark wavy lines with the prongs of a fork. Leave until set. **Cooking time: 20 minutes**

Rich Chocolate Cake

Jane Asher - Author, Actress and TV Presenter

"Good luck with your project."

Ingredients - Serves 8

4 oz plain chocolate
4 oz softened butter
4 oz caster sugar
5 egg yolks
Glaze:
8 oz dark chocolate, finely chopped or grated
4 fl oz double cream

4 egg whites
1 teaspoon vanilla essence
4 oz self raising flour
apricot jam

Method

Preheat the oven to 180°C/350°F/gas mark 4

Required: 8 inch "deep cake tin", greased and floured

Cream the butter and one third of the sugar, then add the egg yolks, beating continuously. Melt the chocolate in a bowl over a saucepan of simmering water or in a microwave, then let it cool slightly. Fold the vanilla essence and warm chocolate into the egg/sugar mix. Whisk the egg whites until stiff, and then beat in the remaining sugar. Alternately fold the egg white and sifted flour into the chocolate mix, then pour into the cake tin and bake for 40-50 minutes, checking after 40 minutes by inserting a skewer into the middle. If it comes out clean the cake is cooked. When cool split the sponge in half and spread with a layer of apricot jam.

To prepare the glaze:

In a saucepan bring the cream to the boil and pour it over the grated chocolate. Stir until it is all melted. Allow to cool slightly. Place the cake onto a cooling rack over a large plate or oven tray and pour over the glaze, scooping up excess from the plate with a spatula, making sure the glaze completely covers the cake and goes all the way down the sides.

Cooking time: 40-50 minutes

Tea Loaf

Christine Dewar - Burntisland Community Award Winner 1988

Ingredients - Serves 8

2 cups self-raising flour

½ teaspoon baking powder

½ teaspoon coffee, mixed with water

1 egg, beaten

1 cup milk

1 cup sugar

1 cup raisins

3 oz margarine

Method

Preheat oven to 180°C/350°F/gas mark 4

Put milk, sugar, coffee and margarine in a pan and melt gently, leave to cool slightly. Sift flour and baking powder into a bowl, stir in raisins and add the liquid and the beaten egg, then mix thoroughly. Pour into a greased loaf tin and bake for 1 hour. Cool on a wire rack.

Cooking time: 1 hour

Ginger Sponge

Mrs Gilbertson - Burntisland Community Award Winner 1998

Ingredients - Serves 8

10 oz self-raising flour

2 eggs

3 oz margarine

3 oz sugar

2 tablespoons treacle

Method

Preheat oven at 180°C/350°F/gas mark 4

Required: 1lb loaf tin

Melt treacle, margarine and sugar together in a pan gently; leave to cool a little. Sift flour into a bowl. Beat eggs into treacle mixture and then stir liquid into the flour. If required, add a little milk to loosen mixture if too stiff. Pour into a loaf tin and bake for 30 minutes or until a skewer will come out clean out of the cake.

Cooking time: 30 minutes

Traditional Damp Yorkshire Gingerbread
The Rt. Hon. William Hague, MP
"Good luck with your fundraising efforts"

Ingredients - Serves 8

12 oz golden syrup
pinch of salt
4½ oz butter
9 oz plain flour
1¾ teaspoons of bicarbonate of soda
1-2 teaspoons of ground ginger

4½ oz butter
9 oz plain flour
1 beaten egg
2-4 oz chopped crystallised ginger, optional

Method

Preheat oven to 180°C/350°F/gas mark 4
Grease and line 2 loaf tins. Melt golden syrup and butter together. Sift dry ingredients together into a bowl. Make a well in the centre, pour in the melted golden syrup and butter, beaten egg and milk. Mix well. Fold in chopped ginger at this stage if used. Pour into the prepared loaf tins and bake for 25 minutes before reducing heat to 170°C/325°F/gas mark 3 for a further 20-25 minutes. Remove from oven and cool on wire tray. Best made in advance and eaten after 2-3 days when the top has gone sticky. Delicious with a wedge of Wensleydale cheese.
Cooking time: 50 minutes

Pecan and Lemon Teabread
Jeanne Rankin - Celebrity Chef, "Ready Steady Cook"
"Best of luck with the Project"

Ingredients - Serves 10

475 g plain flour
225 g sugar
1½ teaspoons baking powder
½ teaspoon baking soda
½ teaspoon salt

85 g unsalted butter, diced and chilled
175 ml lemon juice, freshly squeezed
1 tablespoon lemon zest
1 large egg, lightly beaten
120 g pecan pieces lightly toasted

Method

Preheat the oven to 180°C/350°F/gas mark 4
Required: 23 x 12 x 8 cm. loaf tin and set aside.
Sift the dry ingredients together in a large bowl. Cut the butter into the dry ingredients, using two forks or a pastry cutter, to blend until the texture is of small pea size. Add the lemon juice, the zest and the egg. Stir just enough for it to be moistened through out and everything fully incorporated. Fold in the toasted pecan pieces. Turn this mixture into the greased tin and bake in a medium oven for about 50-60 minutes until a skewer inserted in the middle comes out clean. Remove from the oven and leave to cool in the tin for 10 minutes before turning out on to a wire rack. Let it cool completely before cutting. Store in an airtight container.
Or try this: To make a cranberry and orange tea bread instead, first, substitute the lemon juice with fresh orange juice and the lemon zest with orange zest. Fold in 120 g fresh or sun dried cranberries at the end. You can leave the pecans in, or substitute with toasted almond bits, or leave out the nuts completely.
Tips: Tossing the nut pieces in a tablespoon of flour helps them to keep from sinking to the bottom of the loaf while baking. For extra richness, toss the nuts in a tablespoon of melted butter when they are first toasted and leave for the nuts to absorb this butter as they cool.
Cooking time: 50-60 minutes

Almond Cake

Josephine Quinney - Burntisland

Ingredients - Serves 8

4 oz plain flour	7 fl oz crème fraîche
4 oz almonds	1 egg, beaten
3½ oz caster sugar	1 tablespoon caster sugar
1 teaspoon baking powder	1 oz flaked almonds

Method

Preheat the oven to 190°C/375°F/gas mark 5

Required: 8 inch cake tin.

Sift flour, ground almonds, sugar and baking powder into a bowl add egg and crème fraîche. Mix to a dropping consistency. Spoon the mixture into the buttered and lined cake tin. Level and sprinkle the remaining tablespoon of sugar and the flaked almonds on the top. Bake in the oven for 30-40 minutes or until the cake is firm in the centre. Cool on a wire rack. This cake can also be served as a pudding with fruit and cream.

Cooking time: 40 minutes

Sailing ships come back to the Forth for the Tall Ships Race in 1995
Photograph courtesy of Mike Drummond

Iced Shortcake

Julie Hutchison - Heritage Trust Volunteer

Ingredients - Serves 10

4 oz margarine
1 cup self-raising flour
1 cup cornflakes

1 cup desiccated coconut
½ cup sugar
1 cup icing sugar

Method

Preheat oven to 170°C/325°F/gas mark 3

Gently melt margarine in a pan or bowl. Then add flour, cornflakes, coconut and sugar, mixing well together. When mixture is combined, press into a greased Swiss roll tin and bake in the oven for 20 minutes. Allow mixture to cool slightly. Mix icing sugar with a little water to make a paste and spread over the biscuit base. Cut into fingers or squares. This is an excellent recipe for children's parties.

Cooking time: 30 minutes

Master Mariner Burntisland Parish Kirk
Illustration courtesy of John M. Pearson

Whisky Fruitcake

Ian E. Brated

Ingredients - Serves as many as remain standing

1 cup water
1 cup sugar
4 large eggs
1 bottle whisky
2 cups dried fruit

1 teaspoon salt
1 teaspoon baking soda
1 cup brown sugar
8 oz nuts
juice of 1 lemon

Method

Sample the whisky to check for quality. Take a large bowl, and then check the whisky again. To be sure it is of the highest quality, pour one level cup and drink. Repeat again. Turn on the electric mixer; beat up one cup of butter in a large fluffy bowl. Add one teaspoon sugar and beat again. Make sure the whisky is still okay. Try another cup. Turn off the mixerer. Break two eggs and add to the bowl and chuck in the dried fruit. Mix on the turner. If the dried fruit gets stuck in the beaterers, pry it loose with a drewscriver. Sample the whisky to check for tonsisticity. Next, sift two cups of sale, or something, who cares? Check the whisky. Now sift the lemon juice and strain your nuts. Add one table. Spoon of sugar or something, whatever you can find. Grease the oven. Turn the cake tin to 350 degrees. Don't forget to beat off the turner. Throw the bowl out of the window. Check the whisky again and go to bed.

Cooking time: variable

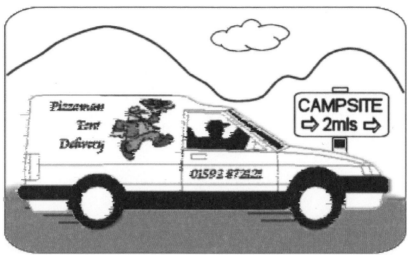

Beetroot in Jelly
Muriel Oswald - Burntisland

Ingredients - Serves 8
1 lb beetroot
salt
raspberry or blackcurrant jelly

2 oz sugar
sterilised jars with lids

Method
Boil beetroot until tender, cool and dice. Fill sterilised jars three quarters full with beetroot. Make up jelly using vinegar instead of water. Add 2 oz of sugar when making up jelly. Pour the jelly onto the beetroot in the jars and allow to set.
Serve with any cold meats and salads.
Cooking time: 1 hour

Sweet Rhubarb Chutney
Muriel Oswald - Burntisland

Ingredients - Makes 5-6 jars
2 lbs rhubarb
2 lbs white sugar
2 medium onions, finely chopped
3 dessertspoons salt

½ lb sultanas
¾ oz curry powder
½ pint white vinegar

Method
Wash and dry the rhubarb and chop into small pieces. Put rhubarb in a pan and heat very slowly. Add sugar in small amounts until juices start to run. Cook without a lid until mixture has reduced, and has a thick consistency. This will take approximately 1 hour. Add the onion, salt, sultanas and curry powder, and finally vinegar. Mix well and stand covered in a bowl for 12 hours. Bottle in sterilised jars.
Can be used to accompany cold meats.
Cooking time: 1 hour 30 minutes

Lemon Curd
Mrs Gilbertson - Burntisland Community Award Winner 1998

Ingredients - Makes 2 jars
¼ lb butter
½ lb sugar
grated rind of 2 lemons

juice of 3 lemons
2 well beaten eggs

Method
Put butter, sugar, grated rind and juice into a pan and dissolve sugar slowly. Do not allow mixture to boil. Allow to cool a little, then add the beaten eggs. Stir again on a low heat until mixture starts to thicken. Pour into sterilised jars and allow to set.
Cooking time: 35-40 minutes

Potted Stilton

Aileen Braid - Heritage Trust Volunteer

Ingredients - Serves 4

6 oz Caerphilly cheese, crumbled
2 oz soft butter
4 tablespoons single cream

pinch of paprika
6 oz Stilton cheese, crumbled
salt and pepper to taste

Method

Cream together Caerphilly, butter, cream, paprika and seasoning. Spoon half the mixture into four ramekin dishes and cover with half the Stilton. Spoon the rest of the Caerphilly on top and finish with a layer of Stilton. Sprinkle with paprika and chill. Seal with a thin layer of butter. The Potted Stilton will keep for three weeks in the fridge.

Cooking time: nil

Pease Brose

Alistair Anderson - Burntisland

Serves 1

Method

Place two tablespoonfuls of pease meal in a bowl and add a little salt and a piece of salt butter. See that the water is boiling. Pour in a sufficient quantity and stir well, making the brose just stiff enough for the spoon to stand in. Sup with sweet milk.

Preparation time: 5 minutes

Jerusalem Artichoke Pickle

Paul Rankin - Celebrity Chef, "Ready Steady Cook"

Ingredients - Makes approximately 2 litres

750 g Jerusalem artichokes, scrubbed, washed
and thinly sliced
3 red peppers, cored, seeded and finely chopped
3 medium onions, peeled and finely chopped
115 g salt
1.2 litres cider vinegar
350 g caster sugar
600 ml water

2 tablespoons turmeric
2 teaspoons celery seeds
2 tablespoons dry mustard
2 dried chillies, optional

Method

In a large bowl mix together the artichokes, peppers and onions, sprinkle the salt over and allow to stand for 12 hours. Drain well, rinse and discard the liquid. In a saucepan combine the vinegar, water and sugar, gently heat and stir until the sugar is just dissolved. Remove from the heat and allow to cool. Stir in the mustard, turmeric, celery seeds, mustard seed and dried chillies, if using. Pour this over the vegetables and, if there is not enough liquid to cover, add extra vinegar. Pour into clean, sterilised jars and seal. Any excess liquid can be reused for your next batch of pickle; it will give it a lovely deep intense flavour.

Cooking time: 20 minutes

Pickled Beetroot Salad

Mollie Sugden -TV Personality, "Are You Being Served"

"Good luck with your fundraising "

Ingredients - Serves 6-8

800 g cooked beetroot, cut in slices
1 large onion cut, into rings
100 ml water
100 ml vinegar
1 dessertspoon sugar

1 bay leaf
4 peppercorns
2 whole cloves
½ teaspoon salt

Method

Place the beetroot slices in a serving dish, together with the onion rings. In a saucepan, bring the vinegar, water, sugar, bay leaf, peppercorns, cloves and salt to the boil. When just reaching boiling point, pour this marinade over the beetroot and onion rings. Leave to cool, then refrigerate until ready to use. This salad will keep for about a week if tightly covered and kept in the fridge. Serve with cold meats fried fish and potato dishes.

Cooking time: 5 minutes

Elderflower Champagne

Helen Mabon - Secretary and Trustee, Burntisland Heritage Trust

Ingredients - Makes 8 pints

1½ lb loaf sugar
1 gallon of cold water
1 lemon

4 fresh or dried elderflower heads
1 tablespoon white vinegar

Method

Dissolve sugar in a little of the water slightly warmed. Cool. Peel zest from lemon and slice into strips. Squeeze juice from the lemon. Place juice, peel, elderflowers and vinegar in a bowl and add the remaining water. Leave for 4 days. Strain and bottle in sterilised bottles. Leave for 6-10 days.

Cooking time: 15 minutes

Tia Maria

Janis Simpson - Burntisland

Ingredients - Makes 2 bottles

1 bottle vodka
3 teaspoons rum
6 teaspoon coffee powder/essence

2 cups soft brown sugar
1 pint boiling water

Method

Put sugar in a large bowl, pour over boiling water, and stir well until dissolved. Add coffee and rum. Leave to cool. Add vodka and mix well, pour into sterilised bottles and leave for two days until all the flavours are well blended.

Cooking time: nil

Caws Wedi'i Bobi (Welsh Rarebit, Rabbit Or Toast & Cheese)

Museum of Welsh Life - St. Fagans

Our thanks to Ian Herbert of The Independent and Mhairi Sutherland of The Museum of Welsh Life for their help and permission to reproduce this recipe.

Ingredients

225 g grated cheese	25g butter	4 slices toast
125 ml beer, or milk	salt and pepper	

Method

Melt butter over low heat, add cheese and slowly pour in beer, stirring until smooth. Add salt and pepper. Heat thoroughly and bring to boil. Pour over lightly buttered toast and serve immediately. Delia suggests adding a dessertspoon each of chopped sage and grated onion, a teaspoon each of mustard powder and Worcester sauce; four tablespoons of brown ale and a pinch of Cayenne pepper.

Cooking time: 10 minutes

Porridge a la Rory (and Atholl Brose)

Rory L'aiguille McEwan - Aberdeen

Method

1) Stone ground oatmeal. (Montgarrie is the best.) Medium or fine, not coarse which produces a concrete-like consistency.

2) A good fistful for each person. The smaller the fist, the smaller the person and portion.

3) Place in suitable pot, salt well . Cover with water to ½ inch above meal level. Soak overnight.

4) Bring to boil stirring regularly. Turn down heat and let simmer until desired consistency is reached. Pour into soup bowl. Add sugar, honey, salt or meal to taste.

5) Fill separate bowl with cold milk and enjoy dipping each spoonful of porridge into milk and eat.

To make Atholl Brose however, simply throw away the meal, retain the water and add a thumping great dawd of good malt whisky. Laphraoig is good. Honey to taste but be sparing.

Barbecue Sauce

Alison M. Rowan - Burntisland

Ingredients - Serves 4

1 lb onions	glass of white wine
1 green pepper	3 dessertspoons tomato purée
1 red pepper	3 tablespoons Worcester sauce
1 lb mushrooms	3 tablespoons of soft brown sugar
oil for frying	½ teaspoon of Tabasco sauce.
2 cloves of garlic	¼ pint of stock vinegar to taste
salt to taste	

Method

Chop up and fry all the first six ingredients until tender. Then add all the liquid ingredients and simmer until vegetables are nicely softened and the liquid has reduced. If desired use cornflour or granules to thicken. Serve as a relish with hot dogs and hamburgers or an accompaniment to any other barbecued meal.

Cooking time: 20 minutes

Dad's Banana Rum
Alexina McGregor Baird - Norwich

Ingredients

2 lb ripe bananas	2 lemons
6 lb sugar	½ lb molasses
hot and cold water	4 level teaspoons ground ginger
sachet yeast	

Method

Put 2 lb sugar and ground ginger in a large basin. Add bananas, sliced. Mash thoroughly. Put 4 lb sugar and molasses in a 2 gallon polythene bucket. Add 4 pints of boiling water. Stir until sugar is dissolved, add mashed bananas and sugar. Fill bucket to within 1½ inch from the top with hot and cold water. When water is blood heat add juice of lemon. Slice lemon and float on top of mixture. Sprinkle lemon with dried yeast. Cover bucket with polythene sheet tied down or with a strong elastic band around pail. Stand in warm place for 48 hours. Keeping it in a warm place, stir daily for 10-14 days until fermentation quietens.

Keep bucket well covered when not stirring. Stand 48 hours then strain into another bucket through a fine cloth bag (jelly bag or pillowcase). Ladle brew out of first bucket with pint jug. Try not to get sediment from the bottom of bucket in the straining bag. Decant into clean sterilised bottles and cork loosely. Stand in a cool place. Rum is ready to drink when liquid is clear. Improves with keeping.

Strawberry Freezer Jam
Marion Larsmirski - Burntisland

Ingredients - Makes 3 lb of jam

1¼ lb strawberries, crushed	2 lb caster sugar
2 teaspoon lemon juice	½ bottle liquid pectin

Method

Put the crushed strawberries in a bowl, stir in the sugar and lemon juice and leave in a warm place until the sugar has dissolved, stirring occasionally, about 1-2 hours. Add liquid pectin, stir for 2 minutes then spoon the jam into small container or freezer proof jars. Cover with foil, then leave in a warm place for 48 hours. Seal the containers, and label them. Then place into the freezer until required. Thaw the jam at room temperature for 4 hours when required. This jam is really delicious and fresh tasting, and best put into small containers and used when required.
Cooking Time: nil

Soused Herring
Alexina McGregor Baird - Norwich

Ingredients - Serves 6-8

1 large carrot	6 peppercorns
1 large onion	½ pint cider or tarragon vinegar
2 bay leaves	cinnamon stick
2 tablespoons sugar	1 teaspoon salt
4-6 herrings, split and with backbone removed.	

Method

Boil all ingredients (except herring) for 5 minutes. Strain mixture. Roll up herring and pack in fireproof dish. Cover with liquid. Bake in a moderate oven, 180°C/350°F/gas mark 4 for 45-60 minutes. Allow to cool. Serve in the liquor.

Cooking time: 1 hour 5 minutes

Somerville Street
Sketch courtesy of John M Pearson

Mary Fairfax, better known as Mary Somerville, was born in Jedburgh on 26th December 1780, the daughter of Vice-Admiral Sir Wm. Fairfax and Miss Margaret Charters. Although Mary went to a boarding school in Musselburgh, it neither gave her a happy time nor a good education, she only spent one year there. She returned home to Burntisland and started to educate herself by reading every book she could find. She went on to become one of Britain's most renowned mathematicians and astronomers, and wrote books on these subjects. She was held in high esteem and many Honours were awarded to her. Somerville College in Oxford was named after her in 1879 because of her strong support for women's education. Mary lived the latter part of her life in Italy and died in her 92nd year at Naples in 1872 and is buried there,

Sloe Gin

Stewart Simpson - Heritage Trust Volunteer

Ingredients

1lb sloe berries
1 bottle gin

1 teaspoon almond essence
4 oz granulated sugar

Method

Discard the stalks from the sloe berries and wash thoroughly. Prick all over with a darning needle and place in a screw- top jar. Add the granulated sugar with the almond essence. Pour in the gin and screw on the lid tightly. Leave in a cool dark place for three months, shaking the jar occasionally.

After this time, open the jar and strain the contents through a muslin cloth until the liquid is clear. Pour into a sterilised bottle and cork until required.

Fizzy Lizzy
Mary Wolfendale - Norfolk

Ingredients - Serves 6
1 pint pineapple juice
dash of Grenadine syrup
1 orange, sliced
ice cubes
1¼ pints of ginger beer, well chilled

Method

Pour the pineapple juice into a three-pint capacity lemonade or water jug and add the grenadine syrup, sliced oranges and the ice cubes. Just before serving, stir in the ginger beer. Serve in tall glasses with a sprig of mint for decoration floating on the surface of the drink
Preparation time: 5 minutes

Tomato and Mint Tea
Hazel Simpson - Heritage Trust Volunteer

Ingredients - Serves 6-8
2 packets of peppermint tea
1 tablespoon of clear honey
juice and grated rind of a lime
1¼ pints of tomato juice
½ pint of boiling water

Garnish:
cherry tomatoes
lime slices
mint sprigs
cocktail sticks

Method

Infuse the peppermint tea in the boiling water, add the honey and stir until it has dissolved. Discard the tea sachets. Add the grated rind and the juice of the lime, leave to cool. Strain the liquid into a jug and add tomato juice and ice cubes. Serve in chilled glasses with a garnish of cherry tomatoes and lime slices on cocktail sticks with a sprig of mint.
Preparation time: 30 minutes

Beer and Mustard Sauce
Stewart Simpson - Heritage Trust Volunteer

Ingredients - Serves 6
1 onion, finely chopped
1 tablespoon of cooking oil
1 tablespoon of French mustard
¼ pint Guinness or brown ale

2 tablespoons clear honey
juice of half a lemon
salt and pepper

Method

Gently fry the onion in the cooking oil for five minutes until soft. Add all the remaining ingredients and bring to the boil. Reduce the heat and simmer for a further five minutes until thickened. Serve hot or cold.
Cooking time: 15 minutes

INDEX

INDEX

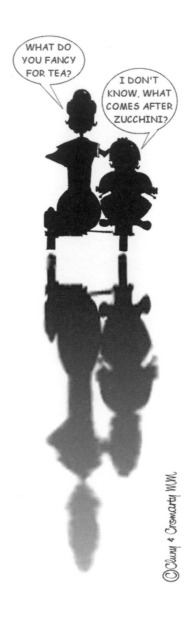